Discover The
Gambia

Terry Palmer was born in Wisbech, Cambridgeshire, famed as the birthplace of Thomas Clarkson who, with William Wilberforce, led the movement for the abolition of slavery. Mr Palmer's school, the Wisbech Grammar, also had connections with Mungo Park, who set off from the Gambia River in an attempt to find the source of the Niger. During his travels in The Gambia Mr Palmer therefore found something of his own 'roots,' as well as a greeting far friendlier than he had expected.

Cover: The old slaving house at Albreda

Discover The
Gambia

Terry Palmer

HERITAGE
HOUSE

DISCOVER THE GAMBIA

First published September 1988
Second edition (revised) November 1989
Third edition (revised and extended) March 1991
Fourth edition (revised) April 1993
ISBN 1.85215.036X
Type set by Anglia Photoset, Colchester.
Printed by Colorcraft Ltd, Hong Kong.
Printed by Kultura, Budapest.
Distributed in the UK by Derek Searle Associates, Slough, and Bookpoint, Abingdon; and in The Gambia by the Methodist Bookshop, Banjul.
Published by Heritage House (Publishers) Ltd, King's Rd, Clacton on Sea, CO15 1BG.

Acknowledgements:

In The Gambia: Mass Cham, ornithologist; Junaidi Jallow, former Director of Tourism; Deputy Commissioner of Police S.L. Jonko, Mansa Konko; the late Graham Rainey, co−owner & skipper of *Spirit of Galicia;* Dr Saja Taal, former under-secretary, Minister of Information & Tourism; Farma Njie, formerly of Gamtours, now operations director Sunshine Holiday Tours; Ray & Mariama Faal (formerly Rosemary Long, *Glasgow Herald,*) Bijilo; and the staff of Radio Gambia, GPTC, Gamtours, and Black & White Safaris.

In the UK: Frank Black, formerly of Clacton Library; Nick Dennis, Hove; Stephen Wilde, The Gambia Experience; Kuoni Travel; Neil Warnick & Linda Paton, Kenley; the group Miguel Villax, Natalie Yarwood, Charlotte Lusty, Nick Dalton, Sam Mackover; John Potter, Knutsford; David Trump, Bristol; Chris Foskett, Bushey; Jean Young, Beckenham; Mike Cadman, Cheltenham; Peter Dawson, Cheadle Hulme; Bobby Quibell, East Sussex.

Titles in the 'Discover' series in print or in preparation include *Cyprus & North Cyprus, The Dominican Republic, Florida, The Gambia, Gibraltar, Guernsey (Alderney & Sark), the Grand Canyon State, Hungary, Jersey, Malta, Morocco, Poland, Sardinia, Seychelles, South Africa, Tunisia, plus several English regions.*

CONTENTS

1: Why The Gambia? 7
2: Before You Go 9
3: Languages 29
4: The Gambia in a Nutshell 35
5: Getting There 53
6: Streetwise 57
7: The Personal Touch 65

DISCOVER THE GAMBIA
8: The Package Holiday 69
9: The Independent Traveller 118
10: Wildlife in The Gambia 139
11: The Nation's Story 156
12: Sightseeing in The Gambia 167
13: Into Senegal 179

MAPS OF THE GAMBIA
Abuko Nature Reserve ... 138
Bakau village 183
Banjul 188-9
Barra 190
Casamance 204-5
Georgetown 191
Serekunda village 206

Administrative divisions .. 42
Bakau & Serekunda 184-5
Banjul area 187
Basse 206
Farafenni 190
Language divisions 33
Soma 191

The   Gambia:

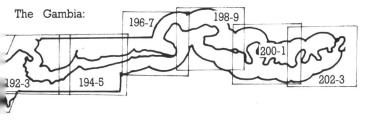

196-7   198-9   200-1   202-3
192-3   194-5

Terry Palmer and his wife Joan pause on a Land-Rover safari in The
Gambia. With them are Rosemary Long, formerly of the Glasgow
Herald and her Gambian husband Ray.

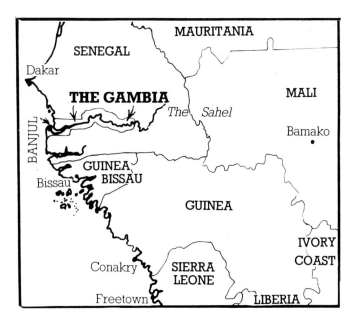

1: WHY THE GAMBIA?

Africa in miniature

THE GAMBIA IS A MICROCOSM, a sliver of Britain's colonial history now finding its way as an independent state, a republic within the Commonwealth.

With 4,361 square miles (11,295 square km) or less, depending upon which authority you consult, The Gambia is Africa's smallest independent nation, with Swaziland in second place covering 17,363 sq km. Big brother Senegal has 75,750 square miles (196,192 sq km).

The Gambia is 29.5 miles (36km) wide at its maximum, reducing to 12 miles (19km) at its narrowest, and is 201 miles (323.5km) long, from Solifor Point, the westernmost headland, to the curved boundary near the Barrakunda Falls, the limit of navigation upstream beyond the last township of Fatoto, but if you were to travel upriver from Banjul you would cover something like 300 miles (485km).

The parallel boundaries of the western part of the country were drawn along the latitudes 13° 12' 15"N and 13° 32' 56"N, though the frontier slips south of those confines along the coast and bulges north of them where the River Gambia meanders through the savannah downstream of Georgetown. This places The Gambia on the same latitude as Barbados and Bangkok, with its capital Banjul on *longitude* 16° 38' W, level with central Iceland. The country's highest point has an altitude of 153 feet (46.6m), north of Basse.

River Gambia. The Gambia River is the heart and lifeblood of The Gambia, which is never called just 'Gambia;' it is the reason for the country's creation and existence; and it was the range of fire of British gunboats patrolling the waterway in the 19th cent which gave the country its unusual shape in a continent of unnatural boundaries. Beyond the border to the north and south The Gambia's only neighbour is Senegal.

English is the official language and is taught in the schools, but the Gambians converse among themselves in a variety of tribal tongues such as Mandinka or Mandingo, Wollof, Fula, Jola, Serahuli and others, which enable them to communicate with their blood brothers in Senegal and Guinea (Sénégal and Guinée to be precise), though those countries' official language is French, and with the people of Guinea Bissau who were colonised by the Portuguese.

Seashell roads. The Gambia is euphemistically described as a 'developing' country, whose people, now estimated at 840 000 are friendly by instinct and who often talk nostalgically of colonial days. The capital, Banjul, and the nearby village of Bakau, which has grown to cater for the tourist industry, are the only places with straight and interconnecting roads, and the country as a whole has just 306km of tarred highway, half of it laid with crushed seashells instead of granite chippings and now collapsing under the weight of vehicles, and none of it troubled with parking restrictions or traffic lights.

There are three radio stations, one airport, no television service although one has been promised for some years, and the nearest railway is 25km away in Senegal across the bush. The weather is hot all the year round (though early mornings can be cool up-country from November to January), with the dry season coming from October to May which makes The Gambia an ideal and increasingly popular winter resort for Europeans, most of whom come from Britain. The country is popular with Germans and Scandinavians, and Spanish and Italians have recently discovered The Gambia.

Most visitors buy a package holiday and spend much of their time soaking up the sun, but there is far more to the country than its 30 miles of beaches, gold south of the-river and black to the north. A visit to The Gambia offers an African adventure at whichever level is right for you: you can sleep in an air-conditioned *rondavel* (straw hut) in your holiday village then relax by the pool with a Martini on the rocks; you can choose from a range of organised excursions into the bush or upriver and see the country and its people in comfort and style; you can be even more adventurous and go by Land-Rover on an adventure trek into Senegal. Starting in the 1993-4 winter season you can buy a package safari in Britain without touching the tourist hotels (contact Heritage House for details), or you can set out on your own by bush taxi and bus, both methods allowing you to discover the real Gambia that the Gambians know.

In this book we look at all these ways of finding your feet, if not your roots, in this vibrant little land.

Compound. A compound is a collection of huts around a central yard. This is the basic dwelling in all the villages and in the Half Die district of Banjul. The concept of 'house' or 'home' European style, does not exist, and you may be asked "How many families share your compound?" rather than "How big is your house?"

2: BEFORE YOU GO

Pills, paperwork and planning

PASSPORTS and VISAS. All European visitors need valid passports, and Britons need the full ten-year document. Black Africans resident in The Gambia, Senegal, and other countries in the Economic Community of West African States (Ecowas), wander around each other's countries on identity cards.

Visas. Visas are not required by British or Commonwealth citizens, nor by nationals of Norway, Sweden, Finland, Denmark, Belgium, Netherlands, Germany, Spain, Italy, Luxembourg and Iceland. United States and Irish passport holders must get visas at the Gambian High Commission in London (☎071.937.6316) or the US consulate.

And when you arrive your passport will be stamped allowing you 14 days' stay, the length of the average holiday. If you want more time, ask the immigration officer at the airport.

Visas for Senegal. The visa requirement for Senegal is different from that for The Gambia; see chapter 13.

Return ticket. All visitors coming by air are theoretically asked to show a return ticket, but this rule exists only because European countries demand the same of visiting Gambians.

CLIMATE and WEATHER

The Gambia is comfortably within the tropics and has just two seasons: the rains from June to September and the dry season from October to May. The rains sometimes run on into October and in exceptional seasons can begin in May.

March is the hottest month in Banjul, and August the coolest, taking overall figures, with little to choose between them. It's appreciably hotter up-country where the midday sun beats down from directly overhead in May and August. In the dry season, when the majority of tourists arrive, humidity is low, but it rises sharply in July and August, so reducing the cooling effect of perspiration.

Harmattan. January to April is also the season when the Harmattan wind may blow down from the Sahara, filling the air with a fine red dust and reducing visibility. Your chances of experiencing a Harmattan are low; your strongest winds will be the refreshing breezes blowing off the Atlantic in the evening, or the offshore breezes by day; strong winds are rare up-country.

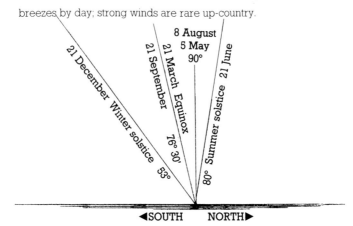

How high is the sun at its zenith at local noon (1305 hrs) GMT at Bakau?

This chart shows the **maximum average range** of temperature, and average rainfall and humidity for Banjul:

	TEMP°F		TEMP°C		RAINFALL		HUMIDITY
	Min	Max	Min	Max	Inch	Mm	percent
JAN	59	93	15	34	—	1	46
FEB	63	97	17	36	—	2	52
MAR	63	100	17	38	—	—	55
APR	64	·99	18	37	—	—	63
MAY	68	97	20	36	—	5	69
JUN	70	95	21	35	3	86	74
JUL	70	93	21	34	10	255	78
AUG	72	91	22	33	18	458	81
SEP	72	93	22	34	11	286	79
OCT	72	95	22	35	3	82	73
NOV	70	97	21	36	1	27	61
DEC	63	93	17	34	—	2	53

Rains. During the wet season most of the rain falls at night, often in deluges, and there is seldom a day on which the sun doesn't shine.

HEALTH CARE

If you go to The Gambia for a fortnight and take no health precautions at all but return to your tourist hotel each night, your chances of catching a nasty illness are minuscule. If you stay for a month in the dry season and go up-country bush-style, again with no precautions beyond your anti-malarial drugs, your chances of falling ill are still extremely small. I've travelled the country from end to end four times, slept in everything from tourist hotels to African compounds, and I've camped in the bush; I've drunk from street taps, covered wells, and even uncovered ones, and developed nothing worse than a minor cough which I might have had anyway.

Expatriate Britons in The Gambia tell me there is a greater risk in having a stomach upset by eating in some of the tourist hotels than by 'going native,' as the hotels have a tendency to practise the risky habit of putting uneaten food back in the fridge.

But if you *do* contract a disease it may be a bad one, which could prove fatal, and there is no point in taking the risk. From March 1989 **yellow fever injections** have no longer been necessary for travel to The Gambia, and all other injectings are 'recommended,' not mandatory. I endorse the recommendation that you consider protecting yourself against typhoid, cholera, yellow fever and hepatitis, and certainly that you take the usual precautions against malaria: don't forget that west Africa was originally called the 'white man's grave.'

Here's a sample of what's available:

Yellow fever. Also called yellow jack, yellow fever is found in Africa from the Sahel to the Zambezi. It is a virus transmitted by the infected mosquito *aedes aegypti* when it sucks blood. The incubation period is three to five days, with symptoms including headache, chills, muscle pains, rising temperature, vomiting and constipation. On the third day the patient may have black vomit — dead blood cells in a clear fluid — with recovery beginning soon after. It is seldom fatal, and that first attack gives immunity for life, or you can have 10 years' immunity from a vaccine.

Typhoid and paratyphoid. The enteric fevers are transmitted by a *salmonella* bacillus passed from the faeces of an infected person by contaminating the water, by being blown onto food in dust, or carried to food by flies. The illnesses last four to five weeks with symptoms that include a temperature up to 104°F (40°C), restlessness, dehydration and the shakes. Enteric fevers can occasionally be fatal by lowering the victim's resistance so that he succumbs to some other and nastier disease. The prevention is in making certain your food and water are clean, but there is also a vaccine.

Hepatitis 'A.' Acute infective hepatitis is a virus transmitted by direct contact from the faeces of an infected person to the mouth of another, by way of contaminated water. Incubation ranges from 15 to 50 days and the symptoms include a yellowing of the skin and loss of appetite. The treatment is a low-fat high-protein diet, plenty of drink and no alcohol for three months. The fatality rate is 0.1% to 0.2%. Prevention is again the better course: make certain your food and water are clean, and think before eating local oysters.

Hepatitis 'B.' Serum hepatitis is much more serious but much rarer. It is transmitted through the blood either by transfusion or by use of dirty syringes. The incubation period can be more than three months and the victim is a carrier for years. The fatality rate is from 6% to 20%.

Cholera. Cholera can strike with amazing speed, killing its victim within the day, yet other people may not be aware they have the disease. Most sufferers go through three stages: thin diarrhoea and vomiting within 12 hours, followed by cramps, a blueing of the skin and loss of voice. In stage two the skin goes bluer and wrinkles from dehydration, and the eyes are deep-sunk. Stage three is the recovery which can be slow.

Fatalities are very low if the illness is treated, but in epidemics among famine victims it can reach 50%. The prevention is, once more, cleanliness.

Bilharzia. Bilharzia affects 200,000 people in the tropics. It is carried by *schistomes,* creatures which live in the rivers and ponds. The female is 25mm long with the 12mm-long male permanently clasped around her. Her eggs, free-floating in the rivers, hook onto human skin and work through the body into the liver. One strain passes out through the bladder, another through the rectum, both causing loss of blood. It's an

The baobabs of Fort James Island (photo: Kurt Graap, Marie's Pub)

uncomfortable rather than a fatal disease, and the prevention is easy: don't swim or paddle in any cloudy water anywhere in the tropics. You'll see Gambians drinking the water from their river, but that luxury is not for Europeans.

Malaria. The ague, jungle fever, marsh fever, periodic fever, paludism, or just *mal aria* (Italian for 'bad air'), has been a scourge of mankind since history was first recorded. And it still is.

The virus is transmitted by the female *anopheles* mosquito after she has mated, and it can strike anywhere in the world, but nowadays it is mostly confined to the tropics. Incubation is from 6 to 16 days, with symptoms being terrible headaches and alternating chills and fevers at regular intervals, hence the 'periodic fever.' Untreated, the rhythm of attacks gradually diminishes but may come again months or years later.

Malaria is a growing problem in east Africa where the mosquito is becoming immune to the drugs, but this does not apply to west Africa.

The cure is chloroquinine and similar drugs, but the prevention is much better; for west Africa take 150 or 200mg of proguanil (brand name, Paludrine) daily, plus 300mg of chloroquinine on the same day each week, starting a week before your departure and finishing a month after your return. The dose is different for east Africa and Asia, and works for about six months. After that it's back to the burning coil, the mosquito net, and the electric fan.

If you're not in contact with mosquitos on your holiday you may consider not taking the four week's dosage; save the tablets for your next trip.

Anopheles. Malaria is the greatest hazard you will face on a holiday in The Gambia, but the mosquito is active only at night and in absolutely still air: your tourist hotel will have adequate mosquito screens on all windows or provide nets over the beds, and you may like to keep the air-conditioning on all night — but in some tourist hotels this comes as an expensive extra. In the native hotels in Banjul and up-country it's an impossible option as the electricity is switched off.

To be fair, mosquitos of all species are a minor irritation in Banjul and the coast in the dry season, and are even rarer up-country unless you're camping by a bolong (creek.) They are much more of a nuisance in the rainy season.

Sleeping sickness. Trypanosomiasis, or 'tryps,' manifests as sleeping sickness in humans and nagana in cattle; it is caused by separate forms of trypanosome parasites spread by the tsetse fly, whose proboscis can penetrate rhino-hide, and it stopped the southern progress of Islam in Africa in the Middle Ages as well as hindering 19th-cent exploration.

The disease is found from The Gambia to Ethiopia, and from Angola to Mozambique, the west African strain being very slow-acting while the eastern strain is more virulent. The International Trypanotolerance Centre has laboratories at Bijilo and Bansang, and your chances of being infected are minuscule. The symptoms are lethargy and swollen neck glands maybe weeks after infection; there's no prevention but the cure is simple.

YOUR INJECTIONS

Immunity. Your **yellow fever** injection starts giving immunity on the 10th day and lasts for 10 years. The latest **tetanus** drugs, and a course of three **hepatitis A** injections, also give 10 year's immunity, while those for **hepatitis B** and **polio** each endure for 5 years, **typhoid** immunity lasts for 3 years, **cholera** 6 months and the *single* injection against **hepatitis A** 2 months. The typhoid injection is the only one which may give you side-effects, such as a mild fever with alternating sweating and shivering; don't make any major appointments for the following 36 hours.

The yellow fever injection contains a live vaccine which is not readily compatible with other live vaccines, such as polio (which is taken by mouth); the *recommendation* is that you have three clear weeks between yellow fever and polio, but if you can't arrange that, a shorter period is acceptable, according to the authorities. The alternative is to have the yellow fever injection on the same day as the others – except hepatitis A, which has a short period of protection. A possible timetable is to have typhoid, cholera and yellow fever jabs, and swallow the polio vaccine, *on the same day,* and relax the next day. Arrange this for four weeks before you go to the tropics, and then have your booster typhoid and cholera (if you decide to have them) and your hepatitis A injection together, two or three days before you travel. The problem is that yellow fever injections are not available at every doctor's clinic and you may have to travel to the next town.

Certificate. Make certain you receive your *yellow fever inoculation certificate,* which costs around £17 in the UK; get your other injections authenticated on the same certificate for your personal record.

Some doctors recommend two typhoid and two cholera injections at least two weeks apart, but others say that one of each is adequate. The official line is that one injection 'is almost as effective' as two.

The series of three hepatitis B injections gives immunity for 5 years, with no side-effects and with complete compatibility, but this is recommended only for people going to the tropics for a long time.

Further information is available from the Medical Advisory Service for Travellers Abroad, on ☎0274.531723; or in *Immunisation Against Tropical Diseases,*, HMSO, PO Box 276, London SW8 5DT, £4, ISBN 0.11.321251.8; or *Immunization: Precautions and Contraindications,* Blackwell Scientific Publications, 25 John St, London WC1N 2BL, no ISBN; or *The Traveller's Health Guide* by Dr Anthony Turner, Lascelles, £5.95.

Other ailments. For me the worst problem was prickly heat, caused by excessive sweating around the groin from too much walking. The prevention is to wear very loose clothes; the cure to apply a soothing ointment overnight. I've travelled hatless in east Africa and Israel, but I found I needed protection on my head at high noon in up-country Gambia. Aids, that scourge of mankind, has reached The Gambia with the staff at Bansang Hospital quoting an incident rate 'of less than one percent.' Sexual temptations are available for men in several of the smarter non-tourist hotels, but the risk is far too great.

An unexpected health problem is an irritation of the eyes which wearers of contact lenses experience if they're unlucky enough to be caught in the dust from a Harmattan wind.

Water. Throughout the country, tap water is safe to drink, though in Banjul it has the faintest hint of chlorine. The problem is that the supply is not as reliable as the water itself, due to the occasional electricity failures in Banjul. Relaying of the city's streets, beginning in 1991 and continuing for several years, should see an end to the problem.

Up-country, there are erratic mains supplies in Farafenni, George-town, Bansang, Basse and Fatoto, with near-perfect services in Brikama, Soma, Serekunda and Mansa Konko. Supplies are usually at their worst in late afternoon, when there's no power and when the storage tanks have drained.

Well-water is available in almost every village along the road, and if you restrict yourself to the closed-top pump-action well you'll have no problems; avoid the open-top wells where dust can contaminate – although I have drunk from several such wells with no ill-effect.

INDEPENDENT OR PACKAGE?

Comfort laid on. The contrast between these two methods of travel can scarcely be greater anywhere in Africa than it is in The Gambia. For you, the package traveller, the country offers a luxury winter holiday in the guaranteed sunshine of the tropics, and, increasingly, a summer holiday as well. Your hotel is air-conditioned, although sometimes as a costly extra; your bed is comfortable, your meals are prepared in European style, and your African entertainment is brought to your door. You need never stray from your hotel – and some visitors don't. For this you will pay up to around £750 for a week's holiday, including the flight but not including evening meals, drinks, entertainment and tips.

Roughing it. At the other extreme, you the independent traveller going up-country will have an interior-spring mattress and air-conditioning only at the Commissioner's Rest Houses in Georgetown, Bansang or Mansa Konko; you will encounter dust and thirst, the vagiaries of The Gambia's public transport system and its collapsing tarmac road. You will cook over a camp-stove or choose from the few acceptable restaurants; you will go to bed by candle-light and wake to the chorus of bulbuls and laughing-doves – and you will enjoy it. Apart from the cost of the flight, you can find board from £1 a night, and live on less than £20 a week.

Extras. The choice is much more complicated than this. The package tourist will inevitably have to spend more than the basic budget as the brochure prices don't include the main meal, drinks, souvenirs, organised excursions or tourist taxi fares, all of which can, but needn't, double the original sum.

The independent traveller can buy into all the organised excursions but is more likely to use public transport at a fraction of the cost but doubling the time involved.

From early 1989 the enterprising adventurer has been able to hire a self-drive 2CV car and go anywhere in the country, but the cost is still high, a comment on the state of the roads. Dare I suggest that the independent traveller who reads this book will be very well informed about what to look for?

The difference is that the package tourist pays for the privilege of having all the problems and hassle of daily life removed from his path, leaving him to enjoy himself even though he will see The Gambia as a spectator rather than as a participant, and he will miss the genuine spontaneous friendliness of the people. The do-it-himselfer (or herselfer; there's no sex bar here) will have to do *everything* himself, learning as he progresses, but he will come away with a much greater appreciation of life as the Gambians lead it — if he can take the strain.

Summing it up: the package tourist buys a holiday; the independent traveller buys adventure.

If you want figures, then maybe more than 90% of tourists opt for the package deal and sample the true Gambia in little doses, day by day as the mood takes them – but the percentage of go-it-aloners is increasing as the lure of the hinterland beckons.

GAMBIAN TOURIST OFFICES

The country's only foreign-based tourist office is in the United Kingdom: The Gambian National Tourist Office, 57 Kensington Court, London W8 5DG; no phone; open Mon-Thur 0900-1700, Fri 0900-1300.

And in The Gambia itself: Ministry of Tourism, New Government Buildings, The Quadrangle, Banjul, but the office deals only with policy and planning and is not equipped to handle individual queries, or bookings for hotels or excursions.

Tourism is a growing industry in The Gambia. There were 700 visitors in 1967, rising to 30,000 a year by the mid-seventies when the first of the tourist hotels opened. By 1984-85 there were 50,000 people coming from Europe, rising to 101,419 in the 1990-91 season – but other sources quote 147,000 for that period. That's Africa for you. The Gambia Experience planned to increase its passenger load in 1992-93, and has also begun year-round operations. Most visitors come from Britain, with others from Sweden, Germany, The Netherlands, Denmark, France, Finland, Italy and Spain, roughly in that descending order. With the start of Air Gambia's services to the United States, that market should increase somewhat.

HOW TO TAKE MONEY

You can take money either as traveller's cheques or in currency: the banks quote exchange rates in the currencies of all countries which send package tourists. There is no limit to the amount you can take into or out of The Gambia, and there's no need to keep bank receipts. You can change unused dalasis at the airport when you leave, subject to a minimum value of £10 in the case of sterling, and there is no ban on your taking dalasis out of the country, but as the currency is 'soft' the money is useless outside The Gambia; even in Senegal you will have difficulty in spending it.

Personal cheques. The banks will also cash personal cheques on your home bank account, provided they are supported by a guarantee card. The cost of cashing a traveller's cheque is D2.

Credit cards. Credit and charge cards can be used in the tourist hotels to make purchases or to obtain cash, with the management

The five-dalasi note is now the smallest denomination available.

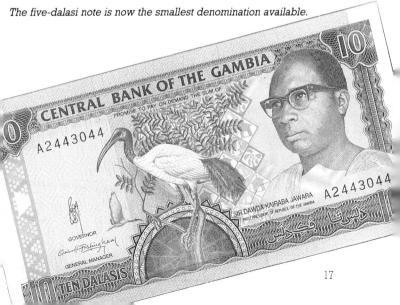

17

taking an extra commission, though you will find some hotels which don't accept any cards and there are only a few which accept all the big four: Access, Visa, American Express and Diner's Club. Hotels are reluctant to handle credit cards from non-guests.

Useless plastic. Outside the tourist hotels, only the largest of the restaurants and some supermarkets will accept credit cards.

Cash transfer. If you find yourself short of funds you may arrange a cash transfer from your bank at home to any of the banks in The Gambia, but this negotiation will take up to a week and will cost 80 dalasi.

Dalasi. The Gambian currency is the dalasi, divided into 100 bututs. Notes, drawn on the Central Bank of The Gambia, are issued in values of 50 dalasi (purple), 25 dalasi (blue), 10 (green), and 5 (red), the one-dalasi grey note having been withdrawn. Coins are worth 5, 10, 25 and 50 bututs and 1 dalasi, but you'll seldom see the smaller butut coins. There is no standardised way of expressing values so I shall adopt the most popular way, with D2.50 signifying 2 dalasi, 50 bututs.

The Gambia changed from sterling to its new dalasi on 1 July 1971, going decimal in the process and tying its currency at D5 to £1, though in February 1986 it began to sink and reached D11 to £1 by May of that year. Since then it has ranged from D17 to D12 to the pound.

Banks. There are four banking firms in the country. Standard Chartered has its head office at 8 Buckle St, Banjul, with branches at Jawara Ave Serekunda, and at Basse; the Meridien Bank is at 3-4 Buckle St, with branches in Bakau, Serekunda, Farafenni and Basse. The Continent Bank opened in January 1991 at 60 Buckle St, its only branch, but with plans to open in Brikama, Serekunda and Guinée Bissau; its chief shareholder is Mohammed Bayzid of the Beyazıt dynasty which ruled Turkey from 791 to 1924. And the Senegal-based Banque Internationale du Commerce et l'Industrie, known as BICI, has the country's most stylish architecture at 11 Wellington St, with branches at Bakau and Serekunda. The Gambia Commerce and Development Bank of Leman St, Banjul, is no more. But neither is Leman St.

Banking hours. In Banjul and Basse, bank business hours are 0800-1300 Monday to Thursday and 0800-1100 on Friday, but in Bakau the banks cater for tourists by opening from 1600 to 1830 Monday to Friday, and on Saturday mornings. Standard Chartered's branch at Serekunda opens 0900-1200, 1600-1800 Monday to Thursday, and 0800-1100 on Friday and Saturday. At the time of writing there are no banks in Brikama or Georgetown, but there are rumours that Georgetown may soon have a branch.

Street traders. But you don't necessarily need banks in order to buy dalasis. Arrow Holdings has several exchange offices in Bakau and

Fajara, open all day but giving slightly less favourable rates. The hotels, of course, change money and traveller's cheques, but give the worst rate of all. The best rates are available at the street money changers, who operate all day and every day along Russell St in Banjul, at the main road frontage of Serekunda market, and at the ferry terminal at Barra on the north shore; when the banks offer D14.20, the exchange offices D14, and the hotels D13, the street dealers go up to D15 to the pound, often giving out mint-condition banknotes — but don't take the first offer you get; be prepared to bargain upwards, particularly if you're changing £20 or more, in sterling, DM, dollars, or Scandinavian moneys. There's a lower rate for traveller's cheques.

Warning. Trading with money in the street has its obvious hazards. Decide in advance how much you'll change, and take it from your hidden cash reserves (your money belt, perhaps?) before you reach the crowds. And *never deal with a middleman;* he might get you the best rate in town, but he'll want his own commission, making your deal a poor bargain.

The black market was originally illegal but its traders, who operate all day, are now licensed. But avoid those at the airport; their rates for a captive clientèle are low. The bank at the arrivals hall is closed? Then try the one in the departure hall.

'Seefa.' As The Gambia is surrounded by big brother Senegal, the CFA franc — the 'seefa' — is freely traded on the streets. In colonial days the initials meant *Communauté Française Africaine,* but they now stand for *Confederation Financière Africaine* . The seefa is the legal tender in much of former French West Africa, now the republics of Benin, Bourkina Fasso, Cameroon, Central Africa, Chad, Comoro Islands, Congo (Brazzaville), Gabon, Ivory Coast, Miquelon, Niger, Senegal and Togo.

DRESS

The question of what to wear, or what not to, is more important for a visit to The Gambia than for most other destinations. The considerations are personal comfort, convenience, and local customs, and you can forget formal wear altogether.

Going topless. Perhaps the strangest revelation in a Moslem land is that there's no objection whatever to European women going topless on the beach or round the hotel pool. Gambians see the mammary gland as a functional organ and mothers quite happily nurse their babies in public, even on a crowded bus. Up country, the Gambian woman's upper garment, the *waramba,* usually has such large armholes that the bosom is continually being exposed, and back home in the compound and around the smaller villages she will frequently go topless.

Erogenous zone. The female erogenous zone in black Muslim eyes is the thigh, and skimpy bikini bottoms are an affront to the Gambian interpretation of Islam. European women should therefore wear flimsy bottoms only in the immediate confines of the hotel or its beach and when in public should try to wear a skirt that covers the knees if not the mid-calf: such a garment also protects the legs from sunburn and allows the wearer to crouch and answer the call of nature — there are virtually no public lavatories.

Gambian women dress in African style, not Arab, and never wear anything resembling the veil or the sifsari of northern Africa, yet they do appreciate seeing European women with heads covered in public: this is no hardship as a sunhat is almost vital in the noonday heat.

Men's dress. Conventions allow men to dress as they please but if you stray far from your tourist hotel in nothing but your white Bermuda shorts and a flamboyant tee-shirt you will soon attract a self-appointed tourist guide whose sole aim will be to talk you into parting with a few score dalasi.

Be comfortable. For those safaris or up-country expeditions, whether travelling independently or not, comfort is of prime importance. You *will* need to protect your head, arms and legs from the sun from mid-March onwards, particularly up-country, and if you plan to walk or cycle for more than half an hour continuously — particularly in spring — make certain your clothes fit loosely, especially in areas where you are likely to sweat.

WHAT TO TAKE

There is no problem at all in deciding what to take on your holiday in The Gambia: the problem is in deciding what *not* to take. Work on the

Casual dress is perfectly acceptable everywhere, but women shouldn't expose too much thigh.

assumption that nothing will be available at destination and you'll not be far from the truth.

For your stay in the tourist hotels take swimwear and casual clothes, and for sorties into the village of Bakau or to Banjul I suggest you follow the hints already given.

Self-catering? If you're self-catering, there's no need to bring cutlery, but see the cost of living and decide if you want to bring any luxuries from home.

Expedition clothes. For those adventure expeditions you'll need harder-wearing clothes; cotton drill trousers for men and slacks or a mid-calf skirt for the womenfolk. Top it with a sun-proof shirt with as many pockets as possible; long-sleeves may be useful if sunburn threatens. Put something on your head, even if it's a woollen cap such as many Gambians wear. And if you expect to spend a night afloat on the Gambia River, take a cardigan or sweatshirt.

Footwear. For your feet, training shoes and cotton or woollen socks *for both sexes,* as insects, the sun and dry grass up-country can work havoc on naked insteps and ankles. Most Gambians wear flip-flop sandals but their toes are permanently bent down in order to keep the damned things on. I hate them, but I must admit many Europeans also consider them ideal; one reader favours good quality leather walking boots.

Equipment. You'll need to keep equipment and accessories to a minimum, but take all the lotions and potions you think you'll need plus, suggestably, a roll of Micropore adhesive plaster. Nurses and doctors are on call at all the tourist hotels but it's still preferable to carry your own remedies for simple cuts and scratches which must be covered as soon as possible. Up-country you must take your own first-aid gear

A money-belt or pouch is ideal for holding passports, tickets, and money, each in separate plastic bags to protect them from perspiration, and either a heavy-duty plastic bottle or a collapsible bottle of at least a litre is essential for your drinking water: take two such bottles if possible. The daily consumption of liquid for an average adult is no less than four litres and it's astonishing how quickly thirst can become a problem. Some people take water purification tablets but I've not yet found them necessary.

Photography. If you're planning to do some serious photography take more film than you need — when it's available in The Gambia it's rather expensive — and carry your camera in a case. A video camera can be a distinct disadvantage and is banned on several organised excursions; you'll find its use limited to within the hotel or to river and birdwatching safaris: see the section on photography.

A rechargeable **electric razor** is much more convenient than a safety razor, and people plannig to spend a night away from the tourist hotel should take a good **torch** or some **candles and matches** – and get them out before sunset.

Equipment for independent travel. No matter whether you're going by bush-taxi to Fatoto or living in luxury at a rest-house; if you're the intrepid independent traveller you must be a walking storehouse for the duration of your holiday. Take your pick from:

Lightweight sleeping bag.

Camping Gaz stove (190gm canisters of gas are available at

Water bottles: If you're travelling by public transport carry at least two one-litre heavy-duty screw-top bottles; you'll not find it easy to get reliable water. On organised safaris or if you're walking or cycling, carry as much as possible.

Toilet gear: you may have to learn to wash on a wet sponge when water is scarce. This virtually rules out the safety razor, and unreliable electricity definitely rules out any shaver that doesn't have its own rechargeable batteries. Don't forget the toilet paper and the spare plastic bags!

Food: as I write, east of Brikama you have European-style food available at Tendaba Camp, the near-inaccessible Kemoto Camp at Mootah Point, Eddie's Hotel at Farafenni, and Jangjangbure Camp north of Georgetown, but I know of two European-based projects which should add to that list. Beyond that, if you're a choosy eater you can live well on local bread, fruit, eggs and fish, to which you can add jam from Bakau and packet soups from home. The more adventurous can sample local cuisine; I've been in a party of four sharing a communal domada in a Soma restaurant – for D20.

Pirogues sometimes offload ships that anchor in the Gambia River.

Don't take a mosquito net. In the dry season mosquitoes are not a problem up-country, and an effective net would be cumbersome.

Walking and camping holidays. For hiking expeditions take photocopies of the best map available of your selected area (see 'Maps'); a tent with integral groundsheet and mosquito net; a hat; compass; and the means to carry water and cook food.

Gifts. The Gambians are poor people and know it. You who are able to afford the air fare to this tropical sunspot are by comparison incredibly wealthy, and the Gambians know that as well. Children everywhere will ask you for money, pencils, food, or occasionally say "Give me something."

The Government's policy, regularly stressed on Radio Gambia, is to urge parents to see their children go to school rather than let them spend their days around the tourist hotels in the hope of collecting a few dalasi. You, the tourist, should encourage this trend by refusing to give money to youngsters — *and tell them why.* There will, of course, be occasions when prudence compels you to part with a one-dalasi coin.

Ease your conscience by putting in your luggage as many gifts as you can carry. Simple school materials are the most appreciated; pencils, for the junior school pupils, ball-point pens for older chldren, plus exercise books or even sheets of plain paper.

Charities. You can hand out these gifts with an easier conscience but it still induces children to beg rather than go to school. The ideal

Photography is a major problem. Children love to pose, but you must ask permission of every adult before pressing the shutter.

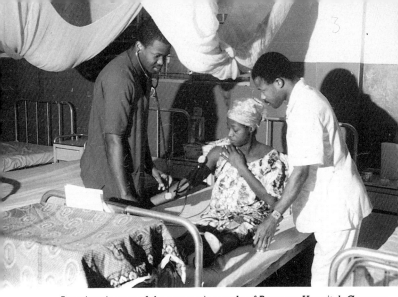

A patient in one of the two main wards of Bansang Hospital. Can you help improve conditions for her?

solution is to present your offerings to the Catholic Relief Service on Marine Parade, Banjul (opposite the service entrance to the Atlantic Hotel); or to Action Aid, near the YMCA hostel in Kanifing, PO Box 725 Banjul, ☎92004, open Mon-Thur 0800-1615, Fri 0800-1300; or to the SOS childen's village at Bakoti, PO Box 17, Banjul, ☎91914. Africa Now has a new community centre at Tanji, needing books for its literacy classes, and indeed every school needs basic equipment such as pens, pencils, paper, metric rulers, protractors, and suitable books.

The Royal Victoria Hospital in Banjul received a £2,750,000 refit in 1991-93 from British funds, and I am pleased to report that due to my appeal in the third edition of this book, Bansang Hospital received in December 1992 a 40ft-container of medical equipment, dressings, and furniture.

If you're going into remote areas, give something to schools or clinics that are furthest from the main road, and note that the excursion organisers give a percentage of profits to local causes.

The lone traveller may wish to keep some gifts as rewards for special favours up-country, preferably handing them to the parents and not the children. A bar of perfumed soap is ideal, but beware that a gift of ordinary soap could offend a Gambian as much as it could you yourself;

and the European-style comb is useless as a gift because it cannot cope with tightly-curled African hair.

CRS and Action Aid also welcome second-hand English-language books from the Ladybird series to advanced science, but remember the potential readership: Gambian schools' history syllabus is confined to west Africa from the Great Empires to the present day, and the children don't have access to computers, microscopes or microwave ovens — at school or at home.

WHEN TO GO

The main tourist season is from early October to mid-May, but the Gambian government has long been wanting to make the country a year-round destination. The Gambia Experience, a tour operator based at North Baddesley, Southampton, has now obliged by operating a summer schedule from Gatwick and Manchester. Many of

---

BANSANG HOSPITAL: an appeal.

The regional hospital in Bansang provides the eastern part of the country with all medical, dental and maternity services, initially working through a network of small clinics in the larger villages. It has two main wards each of 21 beds, and serves 300,000 people.

My first appeal resulted in a containerload of equipment, for which I acknowledge help (in alphabetical order) from: Peter Dawson, Cheadle Hulme; David Earey and family, Braintree; the former Herrison Hospital, Dorchester (Steve Milner, Alex Saull-Hunt); Mohammed Kebbeh, Amdalaye Trading, Banjul; Mr Massani, under-restaurant manager, Fajara Hotel; Carol Senior and St James's, Leeds; Anita Smith and Kettering Hospital; Trolex Ltd, Stockport; Stephen Wilde and The Gambia Experience.

Mrs Smith and Kettering Hospital continue helping with surgical supplies, so I now ask for funds to provide a combined hearse-ambulance, and to equip the mortuary with working refrigeration trays; currently there is no satisfactory way of holding, moving or disposing of bodies, alive or dead, in temperatures which can reach 100 ° F every day of the year. Some funds will be used for transport costs. All donors of £10 or more will be told how the money is spent, and £1,000 could win you a safari holiday, less the air fare. Cheques to 'Gambia Appeal' c/o Heritage House (see page 4) or to NatWest Bank, Pier Ave, Clacton. I can also co-ordinate with electricians who may like to repair the kitchen and laboratory equipment.

---

the tourist hotels close for the rainy season but, given the incentive, more of them will stay open.

The winter is also the dry season in The Gambia, with resultant guaranteed sunshine, except for the occasional hazy day; travel is at its easiest, and there are plenty of birds to see, including several species which migrate here from northern Europe.

Summer is the best time to see nesting birds, and certain river creatures such as the lungfish, but as it's the rainy season some laterite roads become impassable to all four-wheel-drive vehicles.

Away from the coast and the river you may never see a mosquito in winter, but they are more numerous during the rains.

WHO SHOULD GO

Within the confines of the tourist hotels The Gambia is a suitable holiday retreat for most people. Some of the hotels cater for young children, and senior citizens who like a leisurely life would find two midwinter weeks on the west African coast an ideal break.

Wheelchair travellers. The Gambia is not an ideal resort for a wheelchair-bound visitor — but does the perfect resort yet exist? There would be frustrations for the disabled traveller but careful liaison with the tour operator and maybe with the hotel management, should solve most problems.

The biggest hazard would be the steps down from the aircraft at Yundum Airport; it may be necessary to manhandle chair and occupant. The same treatment may be required to get into and out of the special bus to take visitors to their hotels. Thereafter, there are few snags; many of the hotels are bungalow-style or with mini-chalets in terraces with no more than one step at the front door, though most have single steps scattered around the premises to cause minor irritations. Toilets are no problem for anybody able to walk a few paces on crutches.

Disabled people who can transfer from wheelchair to car will have litle problem with the tourist taxis, thereby opening up the chance to explore the tourist market at Kotu Beach, or the African market at Serekunda.

For the next few years the rebuilding of roads in Banjul will make wheelchair travel difficult – but the local disabled manage it.

There are many Gambians in wheelchairs provided by overseas charities, so the people appreciate the problems of the disabled.

Women alone. A woman of any age can safely go alone anywhere in The Gambia, with the exception of the cheaper hotels in Banjul. The only problem she may encounter on a do-it-herself up-country tour would be the physical stamina needed in struggling aboard overcrowded buses or sleeping on simple beds that collapse under her during the night. She would have no difficulties at all on any of the organised excursions, and may find that she's not the only solo female.

Who should not go? The Gambia is definitely *not* the place for members of the younger generation who love the high-life and the night-life of Benidorm.

RELIGION

Seventy to ninety percent of Gambians are Moslems; the percentage varies according to which authority issues the figures. The remainder are mostly Christian, with the few who still follow older tribal religions being recorded statistically as 'animists:' most are from the Jola tribe.

The brand of Islam practised in west Africa is noticeably less intrusive than that in countries closer to Mecca, though believers are no less ardent. Extremely few Africans wear Arab dress and no women at all take the veil. The Mediterranean-hued men you see in Banjul dressed in ankle-length white cloaks are the Lebanese Moslems who run much of the commercial life of the country, and the only woman I met who completely covered her hair for religious reasons was a Canadian who had renounced Christianity on marriage.

Prayers. You will see men on their prayer mats bowing to Mecca at the prescribed times of the day; the exact minute varies according to the phase of the moon, but these are approximations:

> Fajr, at 0620;
> Suhr, at 1400;
> Asr, at 1700;
> Maghrib, at 1930;
> Isha at 2030.

The largest mosque by far is the Great Mosque on Box Bar Road, Banjul, completed early in 1988 on the old football stadium. The former Great Mosque is on Independence Drive near the junction with Mosque Road, and there are a few smaller mosques in the capital, some no larger than a garden shed would be in Europe.

Up-country, only the larger villages have recognisable mosques, a few of which have impressively tall white minarets.

Entry allowed. Non-Moslems may enter Gambian mosques provided they take their shoes off, are suitably dressed (legs and shoulders covered), they ask permission of the guardian, and they don't go in during the five daily services.

Church bells. In Moslem countries, particularly Egypt and Saudi Arabia, the five-times-daily call of the muezzin dominates life on the streets, but in The Gambia the sound of church bells is, if anything, more common.

Although Christianity is the minor faith its presence is strong, with a large Catholic Cathedral on Hagan Street, Banjul, and a Catholic School to the north of it; while the Church of the Holy Spirit and its protégé neighbour St Augustine's School, face the Great Mosque across Box Bar Road.

The much smaller Anglican Cathedral of St Mary is in the city centre beside MacCarthy Square. And in Basse Santa Su at the end of the up-country tarmac road, St Joseph's School and Church stand in front of the smaller mosque.

Bishops. So you won't be surprised to learn that there is an Anglican and a Catholic bishop in The Gambia, and Methodists, Wesleyans, Seventh Day Adventists and Bah'ai are also represented.

The first black Anglican bishop was inducted in 1990 at St Mary's Cathedral, and the president of the Methodists was educated at the Methodist Primary School before going on to the Moslem High School.

Schools. All schools except those funded by Christian sects, teach the Koran, and therefore teach Arabic as well, although this is not a language you'll hear on the streets. The schools funded by Islam teach their students the art of begging, sometimes with practical lessons: catch such a child in the street and for a dalasi you can have a rendering from the Koran, in Arabic.

Coming of Islam. Islam came to west Africa with the merchants of the Berber Coast — Barbary — who crossed the vast Sahara with the camel trains and inevitably transplanted their religion among the animist beliefs of the black Africans of the Niger, Senegal and Gambia river valleys. Arabic never suppressed the local languages, and with the coming of the slave trade and colonialism, European languages and customs combined with a milder Islam became the dominant influences from other cultures.

Koran. Many Gambians have learned large sections of the Koran in its original Arabic and can spend hours reciting it though they have no other knowledge of Arabic — for the truly devout, this is the only language in which the Koran should be studied if its purity of message is to be transmitted. A surprisingly large number of Banjul merchants have made the pilgrimage to Mecca, which grants them the right to prefix their names with 'Alhaji.'

Day of rest. The colonial influence has left The Gambia and Senegal with Sunday as the official day of rest, though Friday remains the holy day. And after marking the Prophet's birthday, currently in September most people including many Muslims, then celebrate Christmas with music and dancing and perhaps a drink of jungle juice.

Ramadan: timing. Ramadan starts at the new moon and so it falls a little later each rear relative to the Christian calendar — and to the seasons. It currently starts in March with all-night drumming in the villages, and lasts the complete lunar month, during which time believers should not eat, drink, smoke or have sexual relations in the daylight hours.

3: LANGUAGES

European and African

THE GAMBIA IS A POLYGLOT COUNTRY in which at least six tribes, each speaking its own language, have merged and intermarried to become Gambians. Children learn their tribal language from infancy and may grow up with the ability to converse in Mandinka (or Mandingo), Wollof (or Olof, Olof, Wolof, Woluf), Fula (or Pula, Pular, Pulaar), Jola (or Jula, Juulaa Serahuli or Bambara; many reach adolescence able to converse in any three.

The official language is English, which is taught in all schools — tribal languages are not taught — but as education is not compulsory, some Gambians particularly the older women up-country, never learn English.

The people of Senegal and Guinea naturally learn French, and those from Guinea Bissau speak Portuguese, so colonialism has done nothing to simplify west Africa's linguistic problems. But as tribal languages recognise no European-imposed political boundaries, the different nationalities converse freely in their native tongues easier than the French and the British do in theirs.

Language barriers. Indeed, it's the European who has the greater difficulty, for there are many Senegalese and quite a few Guineans in The Gambia who know nothing of English; French is very useful up-country and in Barra north of the river, and even in Banjul "Ça va?" is a common greeting.Some of the bush taxis (described later) are labelled *transport en commun,* and it's helpful to know that when speaking French the familiar *tu* is preferred to the formal *vous.*

As Gambian English has a different lilt from British English, there are frequent misunderstandings. A common variation is the dropping of a final -i, making taxi into tax, Pepsi into peps, and dalasi into dalass, sounding so much like 'dollars.' As French is similarly modified, this gives further problems for Europeans to whom it's not the mother tongue.

Portuguese and other languages. A working knowledge of Portuguese is occasionally useful up-country, but no other European language is of the remotest use — except in the tourist hotels where a number of Gambians have learned Swedish, Norwegian and occasionally Danish and German.

Gambians respond well to anybody who has taken the trouble to learn a few phrases in the tribal languages, and you'll find "Salaam aleikum" a useful greeting to anybody.

For a more serious study of Mandinka and Wollof without delving into intricacies of grammar, read *Holidays With The Natives* by Musa Camara, on sale only in The Gambia: try the Methodist Bookshop or the tourist market at Bakau. I have borrowed a little of the vocabulary in Musa's booklet as an insight.

Alphabet. The Latin alphabet adopted for both languages is without **Q**, **V**, and **Z**, but has the ŋ, pronounced as the *ng* in 'long,' and the **ñ**, pronounced as the *ny* in 'canyon' or its Spanish equivalent, 'cañon.'

C is as the *ch* in 'church,' **J** is hard, as in the English *John,* not the French *Jean,* and **W** is also as in English, not the *V* sound of French or German.

A single **A** is a short *ah!* while **AA** is *aaah!* **E** is pronounced as if it were the French *é,* or the *a* in 'hay,' while **EE** is short, as in 'met.' **I** is short as in 'pin,' and **Y** is a consonant, as in 'yellow,' rather than the weak vowel of 'boy.'

ENGLISH	MANDINKA	WOLLOF
Basics:		
Yes	Haa	Waaw
No	Hani	Dedet
I am sorry	Hakatu	Baalal ma
How are you?	Herabe	Jamungam
I am well	Kayira doroŋ	Jama rek
Thank you	Abaraka	Jere jef
Goodbye	Fo waati koteŋ	Cijamma
Good morning	Hera laata	Jamanga fanaan
Good afternoon	Hera tiiñanta	Jamma a endu
Good night	Suuto ye diya	Ñu fanaanal jama
What's your name?	I too ndii?	Na ŋa tudda?
Where are you from?	I te bota minto le?	Yow fo jógee?
Which place is this?	Jaŋ mu minto le ti?	Fii fan la?
Numbers:		
One	Kiliŋ	Benna
Two	Fula	Ñaar
Three	Saba	Njetta
Four	Naani	Njenent
Five	Luulu	Jurum
Six	Woro	Jurum bena

SINGLE JOURNEY PRICES SMALL CAR		SINGLE JOURNEY PRICES LARGE CAR	
KOLOLI BEACH CLUB	50	KOLOLI BEACH CLUB	50
OTHER HOTELS		OTHER HOTELS	
ATLANTIC HOTEL	85	ATLANTIC HOTEL	
PALM GROVE	85	PALM GROVE	90
WADNER BEACH	85	WADNER BEACH	90
AMIES BEACH	80	AMIES BEACH	90
AFRICAN VILLAGE	25	AFRICAN VILLAGE	40
KOMBO BEACH	25	KOMBO BEACH	35
SUNWING	80	SUNWING	80
OTHER AREAS		OTHER AREAS	40
BANJUL	85	BANJUL	
BAKAU	25	BAKAU	90
SEREKUNDA	30	SEREKUNDA	35
SUKUTA	75	SUKUTA	40
AIRPORT	120	AIRPORT	85
			130
EXCURSIONS 1 HOUR WAIT		EXCURSIONS 1 HOUR WAIT	
KACHIKALLY CROCODILE	80	KACHIKALLY CROCODILE	90
EXCURSIONS 2 HOURS WAIT		EXCURSIONS 2 HOURS WAIT	
BRUFUT	200	BRUFUT	250
BANJUL	150	BANJUL	200
SUKUTA	150	SUKUTA	180
TANJIE	300	TANJIE	350
MANDINARI	250	MANDINARI	300
WRESTLING	100	WRESTLING	125
1-DAY SAFARI		1-DAY SAFARI	
SOUTH GAMBIA FISHING VILLAGE	550	SOUTH GAMBIA FISHING VILLAGE	600
TENDABA CAMP	700	TENDABA CAMP	750
PIRANG	350	PIRANG	400
OYESTER CREEK	150	OYESTER CREEK	150
SANYANG	350	SANYANG	400
KAFUNTING	700	KAFUNTING	800
BASSE	1700	BASSE	1800
GUNJUR	550	GUNJUR	600
DAKAR	2000	DAKAR	2300
2-DAYS SAFARIS		2-DAYS SAFARIS	
GUINEA BISSAU	3000	GUINEA BISSAU	3200
PALMA RIMA	30	PALMA RIMA	40
SENEGAMBIA	50	SENEGAMBIA	60
KAIRABA	50	KAIRABA	60
KOTU STRAND	30	KOTU STRAND	40
BAKOTU	30	BAKOTU	40
B.B.HOTEL	30	B.B.HOTEL	40
STADIUM	40	STADIUM	50
SOS	40	SOS	50
KANIFING	80	KANIFING	40
OLD JESWANG	50	OLD JESWANG	60
AIRPORT	240	AIRPORT	260
LAMIN LODGE	250	LAMIN LODGE	270
ABUKO NATURE RESERVE	150	ABUKO NATURE RESERVE	170
DINNER		DINNER	
DINNER	80	DINNER	80
DINNER	250	BRIKAMA	300
BRIKAMA	700	JUFUREH	750
JUFUREH	700	ZIGUINCHOR	800
ZIGUINCHOR	1500	CAPSKRINE	1600
CAPSKRINE	1600	GEORGETOWN	1800
GEORGETOWN	550	BINTANG	600
BINTANG	1600	STONE CIRCLES	1700
STONE CIRCLES	200	CITY TOUR	225
CITY TOUR	4000	NYOKOLOKOBA	4300
NYOKOLOKOBA	2400	DAKAR	2700
DAKAR		EXTRA WAITING TIME - D20 PER HOUR	
EXTRA WAITING TIME - D20 PER HOUR		PRICES ARE PER CAR - NOT PER PERSON	
PRICES ARE PER CAR - NOT PER PERSON			

Tourist taxis are expensive, even when you consider the price is for the vehicle, not per passenger. These are the 1992-93 rates from the Fajara Hotel.

31

English	Mandinka	Wolof
Seven	Worowula	Jurum ñaar
Eight	Seyi	Jurum njetta
Nine	Kononto	Jurum njenent
Ten	Tan	Fuka
Hundred	Keme	Temer

From these numerals you can see that the Fula learned to count on just one hand, while the Mandinka — as well as the Romans — learned on both hands.

English	Mandinka	Wolof
One day	Luŋ Kiliŋ	Benna bes
I have two children	ŋa diŋ fula le soto	Am na njeti doom
It is six o'clock	Talaŋ Woro	Jurumbeni wactu

Calendar:

English	Mandinka	Wolof
Sunday	Dimasoo	Dimas
Monday	Teneŋo	Altene
Tuesday	Talato	Talaata
Wednesday	Araboo	Alarba
Thursday	Araamisoo	Alcemes
Friday	Arjumoo	Arjuma
Saturday	Sibitoo	Samdi
January	Musukotu	Tamcaret
February	Keekotu	Digi
March	Annabi Sukuwo	Gamo
April	Annola	Rakki gamo
May	Annolafulagjaŋo	Rakaati Gamo
June	Araajaba kononŋo	Maamoum koor
July	Araajabu	Ndeyi koor
August	Sungari konoŋ	Barac lu
September	Sunkaro	Koor
October	Minkaroo	Korite
November	Bannakononŋo	November
December	Banna	December
Day	Luŋo	Fan
Morning	Somanda	Suba
Afternoon	Tilibulu	Becek
Evening	Wuraroo	Ngoon
Night	Suutu	Guddi
Tonight	Bii suutu	Ci gudi gii
Tomorrow	Sama	Elek
Yesterday	Kunuŋ	Demba
Day before yesterday	Kunuŋ koo	Barki demba
This week	Ñiŋ lookuŋo	Bes bu aay bii
Next year	Jaari	Dewen
What's the time?	Talaŋ jelu le ka taama?	Njataa tegga?

Family:

Family	Dimbaayaa	Jaboot
Father	Faamaa (faa)	Baai (papa)
Mother	Baamaa (Baa)	Yaai
Brother, Son, Man	Keo	Goor
Sister, Daughter, Woman	Musoo	Jigeen
Uncle	Barino	Ni jaay
Aunt	Binki	Baa jen
Husband	Futo keo	Jeker
Wife	Futo musoo	Jabar
Friend	Teeri	Carit

Same father, same mother. Polygamy, which is still practised, and the extended family system, make relationships difficult to understand. A Gambian will frequently say "He is my brother," but may later explain that the other person is a "Same father, same mother" brother; or is, perhaps, a "same father different mother" brother. Or maybe the two are just cousins.

Food and Drink:

Rice	Maanoo	Malo
Peanut stew	Tiya durano	Maafe
Peanut butter	Tiya dekoo	Dege
Peanut (ground nut)	Tiyu	Gerrte
Fruit	Yiridino	Meñent
Orange	Lemuno	Soraas
Coconut (the nut)	Koko dino	Koko
(Coconut palm	Koko suno	Taati koko)
Pepper (fruit)	Kaani	Kaani
Pepper (condiment)	Kaanu	Kaani
Tomato	Menteno	Cooci tamate
Onion	Jabu	Liñon
Egg	Kilu	Nen
Fish	Yeo	Jen

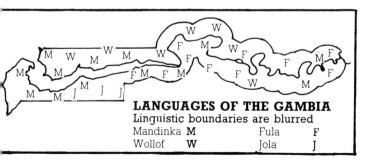

LANGUAGES OF THE GAMBIA
Linguistic boundaries are blurred

Mandinka **M**		Fula **F**
Wollof **W**		Jola **J**

Flora and Fauna:

Mango (tree)	Duta suŋo	Taati mangoro
Baobab	Sita suŋo	Guy
Dog	Wulu	Caj
Goat	Baa	Bey
Cat	Nankumu	Muus
Chicken	Seeseo	Ganaar
Snake	Saa	Jaan
Hyena	Suluo	Buki
Monkey	Sulu	Golo
Crocodile	Bamboo	Jesit
Wild boar	Wula kono sewo	Mbam ala

A word you'll hear very often, once you start listening for it, is the Wollof *Aishi,* (ah-*ee*-shee), spoken to children, animals, and anybody who displeases. Be careful about using it to Gambians, as I'm told it means "Go and urinate elsewhere." More useful is *nanga def?* 'how are you?'

Some of the words in this list have obviously been borrowed from European languages, such as the French for 'Sunday,' *dimanche,* and 'Saturday,' *samedi.* You'll frequently hear the Portuguese word *chave,* 'key,' used in the tribal languages, where it is spelled as *caab.*

The lack of distinction in family relationships indicates the early importance of the 'extended family' or the community as a whole, and the Wollof method of counting in fives is a stark reminder of how simple is our method of counting. Hold up one finger and you have the Roman for 'one,' I. Hold up your hand, fingers extended, and you have 'five,' V. Put two fives together and you have 'ten,' X.

There is little Arab influence on the tribal languages, though some Arabic loan words begin with 'O.' Mandinka appears to have borrowed the Swahili for '7' and '8,' *sabe, nane,* but applied them to '3' and '4.'

Words frequently change their meanings when they move into other languages, as the Mandinka for 'orange,' — *lemuno.* And I like the Mandinka for 'goat' — *baa.* My own first name has a fortunate sound in Mandinka: lengthen the first vowel slightly and it means 'friend.'

4: THE GAMBIA IN A NUTSHELL

Facts at your Fingertips
AFFILIATIONS

The Gambia is a member of the United Nations, the Organisation of African Unity, the Commonwealth, the Non-Aligned Conference, and Ecowas, the Economic Community of West African States. It is a member of the African Commission for Human and People's Rights, with the commission's headquarters beside the US Embassy on Kairaba Avenue. The Senegambia Federation, an agreement between The Gambia and Senegal which might eventually have led to union, collapsed on 30 September 1989 because Senegal thought The Gambia was moving too slowly. Neither country has any links with the European Community.

ARMED FORCES

Until the attempted coup in 1981 when President Jawara was in Britain, The Gambia had no military power at all and relied completely on Senegalese forces. It later created a small standing army, marine, and air defence, initially of just 200 men, plus 400 gendarmes. After the collapse of the Senegambia Federation, The Gambia had a gendarmerie of 700 men who helped the army defend the state and the police enforce the law, but in 1992 the gendarmerie merged with the police.

BUSINESS HOURS

As given elsewhere, **banking** hours in Banjul are 0800-1300 Mon to Thurs and 0800-1100 Fri, but in Bakau the two banks also open from 1630 to 1830 Mon to Fri and 0800-1100 on Saturdays.

The CFAO **Supermarket** in Banjul is open 0900-1230 and 1430-1730 Mon to Thurs; 0900-1300 and 1500-1730 on Friday, and 0900-1330 on Saturday, and these hours are observed to the minute with meticulous precision. In Bakau CFAO's hours are 0930-1200 and 1530-1930 Monday to Friday.

The NCT chain of shops along the country is far less a slave to the clock and opens around 0830 or 0900, closing for lunch around 1300 and reopening at something like 1500, ceasing trading for the day around 1700.

The Foodworth shops in Bakau are open 0900-1300 and 1530-1745.

The **General Post Office** at the south end of Russell St, Banjul, is open 0830-1215 and 1400-1600 Monday to Friday, and 0830-1200 on Saturday; up-country post offices follow a similar timetable but are subject to local variations.

Gamtel, which runs the country's phone network, has its offices open for **international telephone calls** from 0800 to 2200 (or 2300 in some offices).

The ordinary **shop** is open for business whenever there is the likelihood of making a sale, from shortly after daybreak to shortly before dusk, but occasionally trading into the evening by the light of candles or oil lamps. **Markets,** such as the Albert Market in Banjul or the Bakau Tourist Market, wind down their trade in late afternoon.

CAR HIRE

Car hire in European or North American style has only recently arrived in The Gambia, with the opening in 1989 of the country's first **Avis** agency, by the Tropic Gardens Hotel on Atlantic Ave, Bakau, ☎96119 (after hours, ☎91252), address, P.M.B. 63, GPO Banjul.

The agency normally has Renault 12s, but it is impossible to quote exact rentals beyond saying they are expensive, around D400 per day, plus a mileage rate and the tourist tax, and optional personal accident insurance. Payment is by cash or credit card – but perhaps not by every card. **Hertz** has its agency within the Senegambia and Kairaba hotels.

Fritz Enterprises, beside Atson's Supermarket at 17 Kairaba Ave, PO Box 2357 Serekunda, ☎91464, is the oldest-established rental agency in the country with a fleet of Citroen 2CVs at similar rates, payment being by cash in any negotiable currency.

There are several drivers who rent out Land Rovers or Suzukis for the day or longer, *with driver.* They come and go, making it impossible to compile an accurate list, but here are some to try:

Sam's Safaris, Sadibou 'Sam' Jarjue, ☎96649, PO Box 958 Banjul.

Bush Safari, Kotu Rd, Kololi, ☎70611, fax 90023, run by a Belgian man and his Gambian wife.

Montrose Holidays, Bijilo, fax 90023, run by a Glaswegian journalist and her Gambian husband. Suzuki with driver.

Black & White Safaris, Kanifing, PO Box 201 Banjul or ☎93174, 93306. Choice of Land-Rovers with driver.

Crocodile Safaris, ☎96068.

African Adventure Safaris, ☎94034.

Fort Bullen at Barra on the north bank is a relic of colonial days.

Other arrangements. Or you can make your own arrangement with the driver of a tourist taxi, preferably through a taxi controller, appointed by the Gambia Transport & General Workers' Union, and found outside the major hotels. Prices are per vehicle, not per person.

MOTORING LAWS

Your national **driving licence** is valid in The Gambia and you will not be bothered with laws about parking or wearing seat belts. The speed limit in built-up areas is 50kph (30mph), as indicated, but the road conditions in Banjul are a good deterrent to would-be speedsters.

The **rule of the road** changed in 1967 and now everybody drives *on the right*, except on parts of the main road between Brikama and Bwiam where the surface has given way; drive where you can.

Petrol is not always available in every up-country filling station; the 1992-93 price was D10 per litre for 'super,' with diesel at D5 per litre. Unleaded petrol is not available.

There are five petrol stations in Banjul; opposite the taxi stand on Gloucester St, on the seaward side of Wellington Ave by Anglesea St, on Cameron St, on Independence Ave, and at Albion Place. There's no shortage of pumps in Bakau, Fajara and Serekunda, nor on the road to Brikama, but east of there you should fill up at every opportunity.

You'll find petrol at Gunjor in South Gambia, at Kalaji and Sibanor, two pumps at Soma, one at Brikama Ba, one in Bansang (plus a depot that sells it from the drum), and two in Basse.

On the north bank there are stations at Kaur, Farafenni, and Barra.

OTHER TRANSPORT

Taxis. Or you can travel by taxi. There are two kinds in The Gambia; the bush taxi and the **tourist taxi.** The latter are ordinary saloon cars ranging from battered Renaults to near-new Mercedeses which have been licensed by the Tourist Office for the carriage of foreigners. There's nothing to prevent a foreigner using public transport, and only the fare prevents Gambians from using the tourist taxis, for they are not cheap: the D130 fare from the airport to the Senegambia Hotel is double the average weekly wage.

Tourist taxi rates are strictly regulated, and are advertised at the major pick-up points, but make certain you have agreed the price before you get in the cab. If you want a journey that isn't listed, ask around for the taxi controller who will set the price and take you to a taxi, telling its driver the agreed figure. No taxi controller? Then strike your own bargain. Otherwise the normal routine is to take the next vehicle available, unless you have already made a booking with a specific driver. The price is *per vehicle.*

Who takes the profits from the tourist taxi business? The vehicle owner, who is not necessarily the driver, makes an excellent income, and some of the drivers live in comparative luxury, able to forget that the average pay for a Gambian labourer is D350 *per month,* assuming he has the good fortune to have a regular job.

The other kind is the **bush taxi,** but see chapter 9 for more information.

For short-distance travel, why not **hire a cycle?** Rates at the Fajara, the Wadner Beach and other hotels are D10 per hour, D35 for half a day, D70 per day.

COST OF LIVING

The cost of living index was set in The Gambia at 100 in 1974. Ten years later it had risen to 351.9 but in 1986 it had shot up to 693.6.

Confining ourselves to the cost of food, this sample shopping list of European foods, with prices, shows what is available in the CFAO and Foodwise supermarkets in Banjul and Bakau. These shops stock very little that is perishable and in such instances it's better not to look for the 'sell by' date.

The CFAO premises are among the smartest in The Gambia, one on the corner of Wellington and Picton streets, Banjul, and the other at the coastal end of New Town Road, Bakau. CFAO is the Compagnie Française de l'Afrique Occidentale, founded in 1881, and its NTC rival is the National Trading Corporation.

Foodwise has one small and one medium-sized supermarket in New Town Road, and another on Airport Road, Serekunda. This fairly new business is run by a family who were trading in Gibraltar for some years; the owner flies to Britain frequently and buys his merchandise — and his supermarket trolleys — from Tesco in Cheshunt, England, shipping it back when he has a container full. The mark-up must cover the £1,500 cost of shipping a 20ft container, plus import dues.

Tesco's brand name is seen in other shops as well, including St Mary's Food & Wine Supermarket near the Senegambia Hotel (0800-1230, 1600-1830; the shop at Kololi has different hours) and Atson's Supermarket on Kairaba Avenue (Mon-Fri 0930-1300, 1500-1930, Sat 0930-1930, Sun 1000-1300).

Prima digestive biscuits, 300gm D11
Weetabix, pkt of 12 .... D15
Golden Shredless marmalade, 12oz D12.75
Tesco marmalade, 1lb D16.50
Heinz oxtail soup, 425gm D9.50
Celebrity pork luncheon meat, 300gm D14
Fray Bentos steak & kidney pies D39
black-eyed beans, 500gm D14
Blue Band margarine, 450gm tin D15
Delight margarine, 250gm D12
Oxo cubes (beef), 12x71gm D10
eggs, each D2
sugar, 1kg D8.50
self-raising flour, 1.5kg D12.50
Tesco peanut butter, 8oz D17.55
Lea & Perrin Worcester sauce, 142ml D14.75
frozen turkey, 12lb D300
Rothmans, 10x20 .... D65
Lucky Strike, 10 .... D5
Tanga matches, box D0.25
Gambian small loaf D1
– *baguette* D2
British-style bread D4
Snickers choc bar D4.75
milk, semi-skimmed, litre D9.25
Pears soap, 113gm D10.25
Plain soap, no name, same size D2.75
Nivea cream, 150mg D39
Pierval mineral water (French) 1.5l D9
Guinness, 33cl D6
Valdepeñas wine, litre D19.75
Cointreau, litre D199
Drambuie, litre D173
Courvoisier, 70cl D209
Gin, Gordon's London dry, 75cl D75

at airport duty-free shop:

Vodka, Finlandia, litre £5
Whisky, Red Label, litre £8
cheap cigarettes, 200 .... £3.50

Prices are above European levels, yet a large percentage of customers are Gambian, despite local rates of pay: a welder can earn D200 to D300 a week, a bank clerk and a policeman around D220, and the caretaker of the Georgetown rest house gets D1,200 a year, allowing him time to run his shop nearby. A volunteer European surgeon at Bansang Hospital receives D400 a month.

Fruit stalls. There are a few fresh fruit stalls on New Town Road and Atlantic Drive, Bakau, offering good quality oranges, bananas, tomatoes and potatoes. Occasionally there are lettuces, carrots, french beans and melons grown for this trade, and exceptionally there may be a pineapple. Prices are seldom marked and you must expect to pay more than the going rate in Banjul, where a banana or an orange cost a dalasi.

Bread. Bread is available from many outlets. The standard loaf for local consumption is around 60cm long and resembles the French *baguette* but has a soft crust. Selling for D1.25 it's tasty when new but quickly becomes stale. The supermarkets stock slightly larger baguettes which have good flaky crusts and are even more delicious, at D2.50. You can get them hot and mouthwateringly tasty at the Serrakunda (sic) Modern Bakery, also for D2.50. CFAO also stocks very small quantities of milk loaf and granary bread, about the only place in the country where it's available.

DRUGS

The less refined drugs are available at bargain prices in the usual sort of outlet, but the penalty on conviction of handling drugs can be very severe. Do not get involved.

ECONOMY

The economy is almost entirely agrarian, often at subsistence level with spare crops being sold for cash. Peanuts are by far the largest crop, with 74,000 tons harvested in 1990. Tourism is the second-largest employer but takes only a fraction of the labour force although it generates the largest income.

Oil is now the big hope, with possible fields having been located offshore and in the Serekunda area: rumour claims that the Julbrew factory is moving from the Kanifing Industrial Estate to Bijilo to make way for an oil-well.

EDUCATION

Primary education started at the age of seven from 1990 – it was eight – but is not compulsory as the fees range from D250 per term to D600 in senior school, an amount which not every parent can afford. In 1985 there were 189 primary schools with 66,257 pupils.

At the age of 14, children have the option of studying for a further five years at a Secondary High School, or for four years at a Secondary Technical School, with selection by open examination. There are some good schools, notably the Moslem High and St Augustines in Banjul, The Gambia College in Brikama, and the Armitage High School in Georgetown, the Gambia Technical Training College in Kanifing, and the new High School in Soma, but they all suffer from a lack of basic supplies and are in part financed by overseas charities, so your gifts are welcome.

Children study for the General Certificate of Education at Ordinary and Advanced levels even though the GCE has been phased out in Britain, and competition for the top schools is extremely keen: 14,000 children apply each year for the 1,000 places available. Neither The Gambia nor the two Guineas has a university so students need to travel abroad. Gambians prefer to come to Britain for their degree courses but the present Westminster policy puts such severe strain on the family budget that most go elsewhere in Africa, to the USA — or even to Russia.

ELECTRICITY

The public supply in Banjul and Bakau is theoretically available day and night, and is now in sight of achieving that target. Despite that, some tourist hotels and the larger banks in Banjul have their own generators or access to somebody else's, so power failures last only a minute or two until the back-up system comes into operation — but this plays havoc with computers. The current is 220-240v and British-style power plugs fit most sockets — but not all.

Nowhere else has a continual supply of electricity. In the larger villages up-country — Serekunda, Brikama, Gunjur, Soma, Georgetown, Bansang, Basse Santa Su and Fatoto, plus the north-bank villages — electricity is supposed to be available from shortly before dusk until late in the evening; the listed time differs in each village and the actual time depends on local conditions, with a slow but general improvement noticeable. Mansa Konko has power from 0800 to 0200 and it's usually punctual. But Eddie's Hotel in Farafenni has several generators, just in case.

The smaller villages have no electricity at all; the radios you may hear are all battery-powered.

EMBASSIES

Embassies in The Gambia:

Chinese People's Republic: 23, Wellington Street, Banjul. *(You won't see many Chinese in the country, but China has done some civil engineering jobs.)*

Mauritania: 284 Kanifing South.

Nigeria: 61, Buckle St, Banjul.

Senegal: 10 Nelson Mandela St, Banjul (formerly Cameron St)

Sierra Leone: O.A.U. Boulevard, Banjul (Leman St)

USSR: 7, Buckle St, Banjul.

UK High Commission: 48, Atlantic Ave, Bakau, ☎932133.

USA: Kairaba Avenue, Kanifing, ☎562.

Independent travellers who plan to go to other African countries should find a personal visit to these embassies the easiest and quickest way of getting any necessary visas.

FARMING

Groundnuts are the major crop and export, with 128,000 tons produced in 1983. Palm kernel (copra), smoked fish, and cotton also feature among the exports. In 1984 the country had 280.000 cattle, 185,000 goats, almost as many sheep and, in a Moslem land where pork is tabu, 11,000 pigs.

FIRE STATIONS

You won't need a fire station, but you might find it a matter of interest to know there are just three in the country; on Atlantic Avenue, Bakau; opposite the police station on Buckle St, Banjul; and the workshop at Kotu. The Bakau station has a Bedford fire tender given by the people of Wiltshire, England, in 1987. The original WWV 947K registration plates have been reversed to take the new number, G1A 2790.

THE FLAG

The Gambian flag has horizontal bands of red, blue and green, reading down, with white fimbriations (fine dividing lines), but it's seldom on view. These colours are on the presidential guard's ceremonial belts.

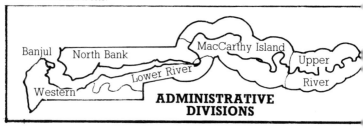

GAS

Bottled propane or butane is available. The backpacking traveller will find his 190gm canisters of Camping Gaz at the supermarkets, and in small up-country shops.

GOVERNMENT

The Gambia is a republic with a single-chamber elected government. Parliament, known here as the National Assembly, has 35 members elected for a five-year term, plus five chiefs elected by the chiefs themselves in assembly, plus eight non-voting nominated members including the Speaker and Deputy Speaker, plus the Attorney-General.

The British introduced elections in 1946, and the first political parties were formed in the 1950s. The political battlefield at the moment has the Gambia People's Party (GPP), the National Convention Party (NCP), the People's Democratic Organisation for Independence and Socialism (PDOIS), and the People's Progressive Party (PPP). As I write the PPP has 27 seats and the NCP 3 seats in the National Assembly, with the remaining five elected seats held by independent members.

Political unrest in 1980 prompted the Government to ask for Senegalese troops to put in an appearance in October, and in November the Government banned the Gambian Socialist Revolution Party and the Movement for Justice in Africa, both Marxist despite their bland titles.

President. Doctor Alhaji Dawda Kairaba Jawara, who founded the Protectorate People's Party in 1958, won the second general election in 1962 and as President took the country into internal self-government in 1963 and to independence on 18 February 1965. The party changed its name, while keeping its initials, but Dr Jawara has retained the presidency. His full title is now His Excellency The Honourable Alhaji Sir Dawda Kairaba Jawara; he has been on pilgrimage to Mecca, and he is a Knight Grand Cross of the Order of St Michael and St George, one of two such knights in The Gambia. He retires at the end of his current term of office.

Regional government. The Gambia is divided into six areas, each with its own council, and 35 districts, each governed by a chief who is elected for life but who can be deposed by referendum at any time if he displeases the district's people.

HOSPITALS

The Royal Victoria Hospital in Banjul is Government-financed, as is the hospital in Bansang; both cater for maternity and child welfare as well as general duties. Treatment is not free for foreign visitors — and why should it be? The sensible precaution is to arrange medical insurance before you come out on holiday. The British Government has improved the Royal Victoria, and I have helped Bansang. The Pakistani community maintains its own private hospital in Serekunda.

Government clinics are in Barra, Bakau, Basse Santa Su, Brikama, Bwiam, Fatoto, Georgetown, Karantaba Tenda, Kaur, Kerewan, Kudang, Kuntaur, and Yarobawal (north of Basse). Mission clinics are in Basse, Brikama, Bulock, Fajara, Kaur, Marakissa (south of Brikama), Sibanor and Somita. There are 13 dispensaries, mostly in tiny villages deep in the bush. They will all administer to visitors if required, but you would be expected to pay what you could afford.

In the event of illness or accident in the Banjul and Bakau area, try the Medical Research Council at Fajara, the Kololi Clinic, or the Royal Victoria Hospital, Banjul.

MAPS

The tourist office issues simple maps of the country – or you can buy them for D15 or D40 from the Methodist Bookshop in Banjul, and around the hotels. From 1993 Heritage House publishes a map of the country, with insets on Banjul and Bakau and with tourist information, priced around D30 in Banjul and £1.95 in the UK, post free from the address on page 4: cheques payable to the author; or from Stanford, below. (Available from October 1993.)

The best map on the market is at 1:250,000, prepared by the UK Directorate of Overseas Surveys and available *only* at Edward Stanford Ltd, 12-14 Long Acre, London WC2E 9LP, ☎071.836.1321 where its price is £7.95.

Backstreet in Bansang. Bamboo is a common fencing material, and most roofs are of corrugated iron.

Good maps are so scarce that the Gambian Public Works Department has bought copies of this book purely for its map; the department should be pleased with the improvements introduced with the book's third edition.

Stanford is also your best supplier for maps of Senegal; the country is available on four sheets at 1:500,000 for £16.50 total; on several sheets at 1:200,000 for £4.95 each; and the IGN series covering northern hemisphere Africa at 1:1,000,000, with sheet 28 stretching from St Louis (north Senegal) to Guinea Bissau and including all of The Gambia. It's in French and years out of date.

NEWSPAPERS

Gambian newspapers come and go. In 1985 there were only stencilled news-sheets, then came *The Gambia Weekly*, *The Nation*, *The Gambian Times* and *Topic* magazine.

In 1992 *The Observer* began publication three times weekly from a Bakau address, and has captured the market. It's a quality paper selling at D4, and its marketing strategy has helped – using disabled people as newsvendors.

British and other European newspapers are sometimes available in the supermarkets and larger hotels, but there is no regular supply.

POLICE

The police force was modelled on British lines and still follows the UK's examples very closely, with men being trained at Hendon Police

The Kalaji salt pan in April. It's too wet to walk on during the rainy season.

College. The uniform is exactly the same as the British policeman wears down to the black-and-white chequered band on the cap, but where the British police now carry firearms and riot shields, the Gambian bobby still has his truncheon — though he has access to firearms in emergency.

Their policy is co-operation rather than confrontation and The Gambia is definitely not a police state; if a policeman becomes inquisitive and starts asking you personal questions it's out of curiosity rather than professional interest.

Outside the capital with its police barracks there are police 'stations,' each with a complement of 33 men, at Serekunda, Brikama, Mansa Konko and Basse Santa Su, and 'posts' with smaller contingents at Kerewan, Farafenni, Kuntaur and Diabugu on the north bank, and Yundum Airport, Kartung, Kalaji, Soma, Georgetown and Fatoto on the south bank.

And I couldn't avoid noticing in Banjul the policewoman who was only a little more than five feet tall.

POPULATION

The Gambia is the second most densely populated country in Africa. This amazing statistic happens because the people are spread evenly across a landscape that has no uninhabitable deserts or mountains. Egypt has 49 people to the square kilometre, Ghana 51, The Gambia 62 — but Nigeria is far in the lead with 103.

The Gambia is also the smallest country in Africa. There are no sprawling cities, Banjul and Bakau are the only towns with a street plan, and the only places you're likely to find a traffic jam are in central Serekunda and along Independence Avenue, Banjul, particularly while the capital's roads are being resurfaced.

The 1983 census showed a national population of 695,886, which is now estimated to have passed the 850,000 mark and is predicted to reach 1,100,000 by 2000. The largest tribe is the Mandinka, followed by the Fula, Wollof, Jola and Serahuli.

There is little breakdown of tribalism as a bride doesn't become a member of her husband's tribe though she takes his family name. The people owe first allegiance to their tribe, an ethnic and sometimes a craft grouping as well as a social division which has been present for centuries; second allegiance is to the nation, with its unnatural borders imposed by Europeans little more than a century ago. But the Gambians *are* proud of being Gambian, and hated the idea of their little country becoming one more province in big brother Senegal, which was the main reason why the Senegambia Federation collapsed.

By the way, the largest town in The Gambia is not Banjul; it's the

Jeswang complex, better known by the village in the centre, Serekunda (or Serrekunda, Serrakunda, Sere Kunda, and other variations), with around 80,000 people. The village has grown from 5,000 since 1950, but perhaps the most frightening statistic is that half the country's population is younger than 16.

POST OFFICE

The main post office, still called the General Post Office, is the large brown building on Russell Street, Banjul, with a bank of customers' post office boxes beside it. The building is distinguished by the smart new Gamtel radio-telephone mast behind it, and the small modern Gamtel office at one end (see 'telephones.')

The GPO is in need of modernisation, its clerks sitting behind old-style counters to serve money orders, stamps, and to register letters, accept parcels and operate the savings bank.

Business hours are 0830-1215 and 1400-1600 Mon to Fri, and 0830-1200 on Saturday.

Postage rates are cheap by our standards, and an airmail letter to northern Europe costing one dalasi will be delivered within four days.

Up-country, there are post offices in Serekunda, Brikama, Mansa Konko, Farafenni, Georgetown, Basse and Fatoto.

Most of the tourist hotels sell postage stamps, but usually only if you buy a postcard as well.

P.M.B, seen in an address, is a variation of 'P.O.Box' and means 'Private Mailing Box.'

PUBLIC HOLIDAYS

The Gambia's public holidays operate on the Christian and the Islamic calendar, and as the Islamic calendar has 11 days less than the Gregorian year, and 12 days less on a leap year, Islamic feasts are continually moving forward relative to the Christian calendar and a person may live to see Ramadan slide from the rainy season, through the dry time, and back into the rainy season again. Islamic dates, marked ★ are valid for 1993 (and 1994):

January 1 . . . . New Year's Day
February 18 . . . . Independence Day
Good Friday . . . .
Easter Monday . . . .
★March 24 (March 13). . . . . Fid-al-Fitr (end of Ramadan)
May 1 . . . . Labour Day
★May 31 (May 20) . . . . Fid-al-Adha (Feast of Sacrifice)
August 15 . . . . Assumption Day
★August 29 (August 18). . . . . Mouloud (Birth of the Prophet)
December 25 . . . . Christmas Day

PUBLIC TOILETS (Restrooms)

There are now a few public toilets in The Gambia. Two are in the newly-improved bush taxi depot in Serekunda, and there are two others in the Abuko Reserve — labelled 'Jane' and 'Tarzan.' A reader claims to have found one in Banjul, but I've not been able to locate it; however, the toilet in the African Heritage restaurant on Wellington Street is almost a tourist attraction in its own right.

RADIO and TELEVISION

Radio Gambia, Radio Syd and Radio One supply the nation's broadcasting; the President promised a television service in 1987, and it may come in 1994.

Radio Gambia is at Mile 7, Banjul, in effect at the south end of New Town Road, Bakau. The name has been taken off the gate and since the attempted coup in 1981 there has been a permanent military guard in the grounds.

Broadcasting started in May 1962 and present output is 15 hours a day on 648KHz, medium wave. The station caters for all tastes with information, education, culture, religion and news, with a strong emphasis on African development.

Broadcasting is from two 10kw transmitters in Bonto, 20km from Banjul, to cover the western districts, and two 1kw transmitters at Basse. There are plans to use Gamtel's relay stations to improve the quality of transmission in the far east.

The station broadcasts in all tribal languages and in English, and as almost every compound has a radio, Radio Gambia claims a potential audience in excess of 95% of the population.

A Swedish woman, Brit Wadner, started **Radio Syd** in 1967 on the president's invitation. Mrs Wadner had established Radio Mercur, one of the world's first pirate radio stations, in 1959 aboard the *Cheetah I* moored in Danish waters. She sailed away when the authorities began closing in, and worked for a while with Britain's first pirate station, Radio Caroline, before heading south — *syd* in Swedish — aboard *Cheetah II*. After a spell in the Canaries she sailed to The Gambia and a more favourable environment.

When Radio Syd moved ashore, Mrs Wadner sold *Cheetah II* to a Senegalese for a floating restaurant — but it sank, and now lies on the river bed a little to the south of Banjul. She set up the radio station near the Mile Two prison west of Banjul where it now operates a 20-hour-a-day music service on 329m medium wave from premises purpose-built in 1977. But long before that, Mrs Wadner had bought a strip of deserted shoreline nearby and established the Wadner Beach Hotel.

For local, and a sample of international news, listen to Radio Gambia at 2200 hrs.

Radio One is a privately-owned music station on 102m.

The **BBC World Service** is available in English on these frequencies:

	0500	0600	0700	0800	0900	1000	1100	1200	1300	1400	1500	1600	1700	1800	1900	2000	2100	2200	2300
25.75KHz, 11.65m							■	■	■	■	■	■							
21.71KHz, 13.82m					■	■	■	■	■	■	■								
17.88KHz, 16.78m														■					
15.40KHz, 19.48m																			
15.10KHz, 19.86m									■										
15.07KHz, 19.91m		■	■													■	■	■	
11.86KHz, 25.3om			■	■															
9.60KHz, 31.25m		■	■																
9.41KHz, 31.88m		■													■	■	■	■	■

Full information on wavelengths and programmes is available from BBC African Service, PO Box 76, Bush House, Strand, London WC2B 4PH, and you should send a stamped, self-addressed envelope.

Senegalese television, in colour, can be picked up in most of The Gambia when the power is available, but there are extremely few sets. Programmes are usually in French and many are made within the country.

RESIDENCE QUALIFICATIONS and BUYING PROPERTY

If you've seen a business opportunity in The Gambia you'll have no problems in getting permission to stay. Apply to the Registrar General of the appropriate ministry (Finance and Economic Affairs *or* Information and Tourism, usually), stating your case, and you'll receive residence and work permits valid for a year and renewable. The Atlantic Hotel, for example, has a quota for one expatriate manager, un-named.

If you're planning to live in The Gambia without working you need to apply to the Immigration Ministry on the corner of Dobson and Anglesea streets, Banjul, stating what you would do for The Gambia. Would you teach? Would you do research into agriculture, conservation, or minerals? You would also need to prove you can support yourself financially. Your application will be considered on its merits and the annual fee, if any, related to your offered assistance. I have the feeling that your residence permit's renewal would be related to how well you fulfilled your promises.

Property. European-style property is cheap by European standards, and is confined to the Cape Point, Fajara, Kanifing and Kololi areas, where a small bungalow could cost from £15,000 and a smart 3-bed bungalow around £35,000. Your new home will probably have a corrugated iron roof, matching that of the British High Commission and both cathedrals, but tiled roofs are slowly becoming popular.

The first estate agency has opened, showing that word of mouth may no longer be good enough to sell your property.

The only other property in which you're likely to be interested is the co-ownership venture at the Kololi Beach Club.

REST DAY

As stated elswehere, but worth repeating: the official day of rest is Sunday although Friday is the Moslem holy day.

SPORTS

The Gambia is civilized: there is an 18-hole golf course at Kotu Beach! But you play on tough grass growing on sandy soil, not on a well-kept turf. If you're staying at any of the hotels in the neighbourhood, ask at the reception for details of temporary membership.

Most other participating sports are available only at the tourist hotels — but some cater for guests whose main desire is peace and quiet. More details are given under the particular hotels, described later.

There is a **football** pitch surrounded by an eight-lane running track, basketball courts, tennis courts, and table-tennis room, with seating for 20,000 spectators – and an on-site hotel, the Friendship, all the gift of the Chinese Governmant. A few tour operators have arranged football matches, but the hotel is in the wrong place for the general tourist market and is poorly used.

Wrestling. The national sport of most of the countries of west Africa is wrestling, and you can either join an organised excursion or, if you're up-country, follow the crowd to any makeshift arena on any Saturday or Sunday evening except during Ramadan. It is an exhilarating sport with up to three matches going on simultaneously and with the spectators, particularly the women, becoming highly excited.

Gambian wrestling is an inter-tribal contest with utterly simple rules: punching is not allowed – that's for the Senegalese – but all other holds are acceptable, including twisting your opponent's loincloth. Wrestlers splash themselves with water and plunge their hands into the sand in order to get a better grip and, as the first fall decides the game, some contests are over within seconds, the winner dancing around the arena to collect praise and a few dalasis while his tribeswomen hurl verbal abuse at the loser amid the bedlam of drums and referee whistles. The entrance fee is around five dalasis.

TELEPHONES

Gamtel runs the country's telephone system and is, like British

Telecom, an offshoot of the original postal and telephone organisation which the British established.

International calls. You can call home at any time of the day or night from an office near the Atlantic Hotel in aptly-named Telegraph Road, Banjul, and from any of four kiosks inside the Gamtel office on Russell St, beside the GPO building. These are the only public international phones which are always open.

You can also make that call home between 0800 and 2400 from the Gamtel offices on Atlantic Ave, Bakau; by the Bungalow Beach Hotel, Kotu; near the Senegambia Hotel; at the south end of Kairaba Ave, Serekunda; at Yundum Airport; and in Bansang, Barra, Basse Santa Su, Brikama, Farafenni, Fatoto, Serekunda main road and Soma. Every Gamtel office now has a **fax machine,** with a single-sheet internal transmission costing around D5, or D25 to Europe.

Cost. The cost of a phone call is D26 a minute to Europe Mon-Fri 0600-1800; D20 Mon-Fri 1800-2300; and D16 Mon-Fri 2300-0600, plus Sat and Sun. Smart cards cost D45. You can, of course, phone from your tourist hotel and pay the extra commission.

If you would like a return call at a Gamtel office, ask the desk clerk your kiosk number before you dial out. Bakau numbers begin with 95, Serekunda with 92 or 93, Banjul with 26, 27, 28 or 29, and there are **no area codes** in the country.

The system uses satellite communication which came into operation on 25 April 1978 from an earth station at Abuko. The quality of reception is excellent, and there is speculation that cellphones may soon be introduced.

International codes. To make an international call, first dial **000,** then the code of the country you are calling:

Australia	61
Belgium	32
Canada	1
Denmark	45
Finland	251
France	33
Germany	49
Ireland	353
Italy	39
Netherlands	31
New Zealand	64
Norway	47
Sweden	46
Switzerland	41
USA	1
United Kingdom	44

National and local calls. Calls within The Gambia are another matter, as this part of the system is still being modernised and depends on ancient gear inherited from the British, and up-country repeater stations. Reception, even over two or three miles, is occasionally poor and, until recently, government clerks would carry messages on paper from office to office rather than rely on the phone.

To make a local call from any kiosk, insert 25 or 50 butut or 1 dalasi coins into a visible slot, then dial the number; a single pulse, half the speed of the British 'engaged' tone, is the call tone. Your coins start disappearing as soon as your call is answered, and you automatically get back any unusued coins when you replace the receiver.

TIME
The Gambia is on Greenwich Mean Time all the year. Being so close to the equator there is no appreciable difference in the length of daylight which is approximately 12 hours every day – from 0700 to 1900. You might expect sunrise at 0600, but Banjul's longidude of 16° 38' W of Greenwich explains the delay.

WEIGHTS and MEASURES
Gambians use metric measures, but there is still a lingering use of the Imperial system with weights although petrol and beer are sold by the litre. In 1991 kilometer marker posts were put in beside the tarmac road on the south bank.

Few up-country bush taxis are this smart. The man in the white hat is a popular broadcaster on Radio Gambia.

5: GETTING THERE

Land, sea or air

NORMALLY, THERE ARE THREE WAYS of getting to The Gambia, but in 1990-91 only 1,710 people came by cruise liner – and in 1992 all trans-Sahara land crossing was made impossible by armed bandits in southern Algeria.

AIR

Air travel is, understandably, the most popular, with charter flights now available from Manchester and London (Gatwick) year-round; other charters, winter-only, operate from Germany, Denmark, France, Sweden, Italy and Spain, with Switzerland coming onto the list.

Air Gambia. Scheduled flights include Air Gambia's Boeing 707-300 to Gatwick, and on to Freetown; the company began operations in March 1991 and from August 1992 to New York as well. The airline is jointly owned by three Gambian businessmen and Omega Air of Dublin, which also owns the aircraft. Initially its planes are serviced at Manston, Kent, but the company wants to open a maintenance hangar at Yundum to serve other airlines as well as itself.

Contacts: Suite 225, Ashdown House, Gatwick Airport, RH6 0DW, ☎0293.507333; 7-9 Nelson Mandela St, PO Box 149, Banjul, ☎27824.

Gambia Airways. The name 'Gambia Airways' has been around for several years; at last the company has got airborne, with YS11 turbo-prop aircraft serving Nouakchott, Dakar, Bissau, Conakry and Freetown. Office: 16-17 Wellington St, Banjul, ☎27778.

The Gambia Air Shuttle, the country's first attempt at establishing a national airline, collapsed in 1990, and the new companies have no connection with it or its directors.

Yundum Airport – Arrival. The terminal building at Yundum Airport (BJL for 'Banjul' on your luggage labels) was built with a loan from Britain, and opened by President Dawda Jawara on 24 April 1977. It is capable of handling one flight at a time although it is now called upon to handle two within 20 minutes, and it has the minimum of services: a tiny outdoor kiosk serving as the currency change office for incoming flights (if it's closed, try the office in the departure hall rather than the money changers outside). There is neither restaurant nor toilet, and the Gamtel office is a separate building outside.

As an arriving visitor you leave the plane by a staircase and walk around 250 metres across the apron to the terminal. There is a simple passport check, you hand in the landing card and questionnaire you completed on the plane, then collect your luggage in the bright African sunshine. A customs officer may want to rummage in your luggage before he chalks his 'X' – and you are free to enter The Gambia.

This is where the independent traveller has his first shock, as package tourists climb into their luxury coaches. There is no car rental agency and no bus service, leaving the option of taking a tourist taxi to Bakau for D240 (several people can share the taxi and the fare), or walking the mile to the main road and catching a bush taxi for D4.

You will find several baggage handlers willing to help you with your luggage in return for a tip; D20 is adequate for normal bags although you may be asked for D100. You will need to change some money at the tiny bank.

Yundum Airport – Departure. The options for travel are the same but, once in the airport, departing travellers have a good toilet, a duty-free shop, a post office and a small bar, but as the terminal is far too small for the traffic it faces, the Belgian and Japanese governments have offered to finance its expansion.

You will pass through a security arch, but your luggage will be searched by hand, so ushering you through to the smart departure lounge. The duty free shop opens an hour before take-off, selling cigarettes, perfumes and spirits, but at prices seldom better than those in the supermarkets.

Baggage reclaim. Finally, your baggage will be spread out neatly on the tarmac for you to identify; a small tip will exempt you from any customs search.

Departure tax. Several readers have reported the £7 departure tax for foreigners (D35 for Gambians) but I have never been asked for it.

SEA

At the time of writing, no shipping line takes passengers from northern Europe to Banjul, but the Grimaldi Line operates a limited passenger service to Dakar; contact any freight forwarding agency for the latest information.

A limited number of cruise liners call at Banjul; your travel agent will have details.

OVERLAND

In 1992 armed bandits in southern Algeria began robbing convoys crossing the southern Sahara. Add the problems with Polisario in the former Spanish Sahara and you have closed all four motor routes through the desert. For the latest information contact the Foreign Office Travel Advice Unit, ☎071.270.4129.

Yundum Airport departure lounge between flights. Tables and chairs are now available.

AN UNUSUAL ARTIST

Joseph Morkeh-Yamson Jr is a Sierra Leonian exile who has lived in Kololi village since 1985; he went to primary school in Golder's Green, London.

A graphic designer in a land with no use for his skills, he has turned to art to make his living, with a range of styles from abstract and surrealist to near-photographic precision, in water colour or oils. He has exhibited at the African Heritage gallery, Banjul, but relies mainly on recommendation and chance sales with prices from £20.

You can reach Joe on PMB 368 Serekunda or ☎27372, and ask for Mrs Jane Clement. Joe lives beside the *church* — not a mosque — in Kololi.

Not coconuts – kola nuts. Kola and the coca plant were among the ingredients in a well-known soft drink, above; below, the BICI bank in Banjul has The Gambia's most revolutionary architecture.

6: STREETWISE

Your key to 'instant experience'

BARGAINING

There is surprisingly little scope in The Gambia to show your skills in bargaining. The tourist taxi fares are set by the Government and shown on notices outside the gates of most of the tourist hotels; sometimes they're even displayed in the reception area. The stallholders on New Town Road and Atlantic Boulevard, Bakau, seldom publicise the price of their fruit but they'll only consider bargaining if they have anything that looks as if it won't be fit for sale by the end of the day. The stallholders in Albert Market, Banjul, are working on a fairly slender profit margin and are handling durable goods that certainly *will* be saleable the next day.

That leaves only the craftsmen in the souvenir market at Kotu Beach, and the traders who come into the hotel grounds during the evenings to sell their woodcarvings or batik shirts. They will usually open the bidding by asking twice the expected closing price, and if trade is slow they'll try to stimulate interest by making the first reduction.

After that, it's up to you. Start your bidding at 20% of the asking price, and go up slower than the seller comes down. Settle early if you want to be generous, but if you force the price to the half-way mark or beneath, consider yourself morally obliged to buy.

CRIME ON THE STREETS

The Gambia is one of the safest countries in Black Africa for a white man and you will certainly be safer walking the darkened streets of Banjul at 9pm than you would in almost any city in Europe or North America. And up-country in Georgetown or beyond it would be inconceivable for a Gambian to attack you by day or by night.

That doesn't mean there is no crime or that there's no need to be cautious: it merely reinforces the argument that in a society where everybody is poor, the crime rate is low. The worst place is aboard the Banjul-Barra ferry where pickpockets take advantage of the crowds; backpackers beware.

Reader Chris Foskett, on a guided tour, reports: "We experienced a nasty incident in Serekunda market. We were told to keep together, but two men got among us and tried to steal from one of the girls' shoulder bag. What amazed us was the reaction of the other stallholders; they were furious, apologising profusely to us and dealing with the culprits *very* roughly. Some time later we saw them again, still dealing out their own punishment."

There *is* crime. In 1988 one incident in particular aroused public indignation. Some people alleged to have been from Guinea Bissau drove up in a large van to an unoccupied European-style house in Bakau and emptied of its furniture. I have met a well-built white man who was attacked and robbed in Bund Road, Banjul – the road across the marshes and an obvious ambush – and I have reports of a hold-up in Clarkson St late at night. Serious crime is nonetheless rare.

Murder. There are even a few murderers on the run: look in any of the up-country police stations and you'll see their identity-card photographs in rogues' alley beneath that ominous word 'Wanted.' But these are crimes of passion by blacks against blacks, or of family feuds, and the criminal's only hope of avoiding capture is to flee the country.

Extended family. Throughout Black Africa, and indeed in many other parts of the world where poverty is a way of life, every wage-earner is expected to help support anybody else in the family who has fallen upon hard times. This 'extended family' system is a kind of voluntary social security which provides everybody with the basic requirements of life: food, shelter and clothing.

Banjul is a poor city with many compounds built of corrugated iron and with communal taps at the street corners, but its people are honest. Dakar is a modern metropolis with gleaming high-rise buildings and a cost of living to match — and its crime rate is phenomenal. If you venture into Dakar alone, be on your guard all the time, don't wander down any back-alleys, and on no account agree to go into any building with anybody you meet on the street: this is a common way of setting up the victim who will be stripped clean of everything of value.

Opportunism. The crime of opportunism is much more prevalent as I learned when inspecting a cycle for hire in Bakau. A young man in a red tee-shirt asked if I was interested, then he pointed out the brakes, the combination lock, and took my money for the rental. I was about to ride away when the proprietor asked me what I was doing; the man in the red tee-shirt had quietly and expertly disappeared. The moral is obvious: *in any dealings, make certain you pay the right person and avoid the middle-man.* This applies equally to the youth who knows somebody who can get you something cheap, or who will arrange a taxi for you, or who will change your money for you on the black market.

PROSTITUTION

Prostitution has long been illegal in The Gambia, but a leading journalist told me of a proposal to reclassify prostitutes as 'sexual workers' and tax them.

This pirogue, being built at Barra, will go to sea with its overlong keel.

Illegal or not, a few sexual workers have been employed in Banjul for many years but, I am told, Gambian women are almost never involved because the city is too small to preserve their anonymity, and so French-speaking Senegalese beauties have the market. There is no prostitution on the streets, nor is there a red-light district; the girls operate discreetly — for example, by knocking on my door at midnight when I was staying alone in a certain Banjul hotel which has now ceased this trade.

Mr Tabar, owner of Eddie's Hotel in Farafenni, told me that several Senegalese beauties gather in the hotel's secluded garden each evening and are available at a price — don't ask me how much; I don't know. But I can report that the girls are really beautiful.

Homosexual. Homosexual approaches are rare but I had one whispered offer: "You want a poofter?" I did not.

PHOTOGRAPHY

There are two distinct problems facing the photographer in The Gambia: children who demand to be photographed, and elders who refuse to be. After numerous visits to The Gambia, with still and video cameras, after being arrested for filming, and after discussing photography with a cross-section of Gambians, I believe I can understand Gambian attitudes.

Rules on photography. The unwritten rules first demand that you *always* ask permission of anybody likely to be in front of your lens when you press the shutter; you should respect a refusal, and give something if asked. Don't photo any private property without the owner's consent: this includes homes, trees, cattle, and fishing canoes.

Given consent to photo one subject, don't assume the permission covers other subjects. For example, I gave pencils and paper to children in a remote up-country village, and was then free to film them around our Land-Rover − but I asked permission to turn the camera on the village huts and the river.

Be very careful in crowded places, such as Banjul city and Serekunda market. In these places it's not enough to film or photograph your companion, as too many other people invariably walk into the picture. Either do it surreptitiously, or don't do it at all.

Filming in crowded areas is much easier if you happen to be black, or if you are obviously in the company of black people, but white visitors must always remember that courtesy is essential. I have filmed a Moslem wedding in Bijilo village with no problems − because I was shown around by a man from the village.

Police. On my second visit to The Gambia I had a letter of authority from the Ministry of Tourism, but it did not relieve me of the need to ask permission. I was arrested in Georgetown for filming the ferry and catching a man who walked into camera shot waving his arm in protest. As this happened outside the police station I had some awkward moments, was threatened with confiscation of my tape, and I soothed the situation only with deep apologies.

Georgetown's northern ferry. I was arrested here for filming a man without his permission: see the text.

After this experience I strongly advise asking the local police for permission to film or photograph, as a matter of courtesy − it also helps if you're challenged by an angry citizen − but it is not in the police mandate to grant or refuse permission, although the police will uphold the right of an individual who does not want to be filmed.

Finally, try to see the situation from the Gambian viewpoint. Gambians are poor, and know it; *toubabs* are very rich (they can afford the air fare, can't they?). Cameras are *very* expensive, and a video camera can cost five years' pay. Why should the *toubabs* use their very expensive equipment to capture the black man's poverty − particularly without asking or paying for the privilege? It is inexcusably offensive to photograph the poorest areas, such as Bakau native village: don't even consider taking your camera there.

This makes for near-impossible conditions if you want to take street scenes, or shots in the crowded Serekunda or Bakau produce markets; I found the solution to be the pre-focused snatch shot with the camera held at chest level, or by using a telephoto lens from some hidden vantage-point. Another option is to photo other persons in your party but have the background as the point of interest.

Neither of these solutions provides the perfect answer, and I have had shouts of protest from people a hundred yards away who suspected a long-focus lens was pointing in their direction; usually they were correct.

My strangest experience with an objector happened in Gloucester Street, Banjul, when I zoomed the telephoto lens onto the exotic blossom on a tree. As I was about to press the shutter a man shouted: "No! You may not photograph that tree! It is mine!"

Video cameras. Reactions to video cameras are even more exaggerated than they are to still cameras. The children gather as if around a Pied Piper, but adults react even more strongly, which is why video cameras are banned on several of the organised excursions.

While on the subject of photography it's worth noting that The Gambia has other problems for the amateur cameraman. The scenery lacks the grandeur of mountain, cliff or desert, and when you have photographed one village or one bend in the river, you have done them all. There are, nonetheless, some beautiful shots to be captured: I have an enlargement of the Fatoto ferry hanging on my office wall.

POLICE CHECKS

The police at the tiny village of Kalaji, three-quarters of the distance from Banjul to Soma along the tarmac road, stop and check all traffic except GPTC buses and tourist coaches as a routine procedure, and police at other up-country stations occasionally check everything, asking to see proof of identity of all Africans present but seldom bothering the Europeans. This is a result of the attempted coup in 1981, and the police claim they are looking for arms, but all I saw confiscated was a bottle of lotion for making the complexion paler; this particular product is banned because it has suspected carcinogenic ingredients.

On one occasion when a crowded bus was delayed for half an hour several passengers had a heated argument with the police, further evidence that The Gambia is not ruled by its police force.

Police checks can be set up anywhere, and expatriates have told me of three at the same time in Kairaba Avenue, with officers looking for the smallest defect in a vehicle — not difficult with most vehicles. Gambians cynically say the police 'need to feed their families'.

SOUVENIRS

The Gambian woodcarvers produce some wonderful souvenirs, usually life-size masks of the type that were formerly found in tribal ceremonies. The only trouble with them is that they are often just too big to squeeze into your luggage for the homeward flight.

Batik. Batik and tie-dying are popular, and you can tour the tiny workshop near Cape Point where ordinary cotton shirts are transformed into dazzling colours.

Gold and silver. West African craftsmen have been producing excellent precious metal ware for centuries, though the cost of the raw material limits its use these days. Gold was known to the Africans long before the Berbers crossed the Sahara Desert and traded the metal for salt on a weight-for-weight basis; the lure of gold brought the first Europeans to the area they called the Gold Coast, now Ghana, and the gold deposits of Guinea and Guinea Bissau went to make the golden guinea coins that helped to build the economies of western Europe.

Wood carvings. Most of the woodcarvers in The Gambia belong to a small group of families which has passed the craft down through the male line for many generations, the boys starting to learn their life's work as soon as they reach adolescence. Their carving is of superb quality and is on sale in the *bengdulas* or craft markets at Bakau, the Senegambia, Kotu Beach, at the airport, and at many hotels, but you should visit the market at Brikama where most of the carvers work.

Trading in ivory, skins, or any other animal derivatives is banned, and you face possible prosecution if you try exporting such items.

TIPPING

I never know how much or how little to tip so I am grateful to Wings for the suggestion of a D5 tip to an excursion driver or guide for a full day's outing, or D3 for a half day — per couple. At a tourist-class restaurant you should tip around 5% provided there is no service charge on the bill. Try to give it to the waiter to make certain he gets it.

I feel that the fares set for the tourist taxis are already high enough

An antelope takes shape in the expert hands of this Brikama woodcarver.

and that no further payment is warranted unless you have received exceptional service.

Outside the tourist circuit no European is expected to provide a tip as a matter of routine, but you should, of course, acknowledge anybody who has helped you. This brings us into the complicated field of gifts, and I suggest the procedure should be to offer some small luxury such as a bar of perfumed soap or a present for the children.

TOURIST GUIDES

You will quickly realise there are two types of tourist guide: the one you want, and the one you don't. There are very few of the first type; people such as Mass Cham the bird man, and the guides who come with the organised excursions. They have their set fees, they can be contacted through the hotels or the tour operators, and they don't pester you.

Self-appointed guides. The other type of tourist guide is self-appointed and will often claim to be 'well-known at the X Hotel,' though there is a reluctance to say why he is well-known. These young men are a natural product of the culture clash between the affluent tourist and the penniless local and are to be found throughout the poorer lands...and in a few of the not so poor, as well.

I know of no foolproof method of dissuading him he is not wanted, but I do know you cannot buy him off: "Here's twenty dalasi if you go away." No; he will want D30, or D40. Once your guide has appointed himself you and he are engaged in a battle of wits and you both know you are going to be the loser.

The answer lies in recognising the type of victim the self-appointed guide looks for. The lone male traveller or the couple; he is deterred by three or more people. And he seldom chooses a lone female as he could be accused of molesting her. He looks for the person who is hesitant, who is not walking purposefully, and preferably the person who looks the typical tourist, with bright shirt and shorts and a gay sun hat.

Often on my solo travels I stop and take notes or photographs, which makes me a prime target. I have tried misunderstanding English, being tired, being without money, but I eventually found the only remedy was to tell the truth: "I don't want you. You're my friend, yes — but go away."

It's so easy to be permanently on the defensive and miss the genuine approach purely out of friendship, particularly in the Upper River Division where you can make what appears to be a lifelong friendship half an hour after first meeting.

Or perhaps you are happy with a self-appointed guide? I have had reports of visitors being shown things they would otherwise have missed, of being taken to the compound to meet the family, taken to naming ceremonies (the Moslem equivalent of a christening), helped to bargain in the markets — and protected from other such guides. If you would like the services of such a guide, strike a bargain at the outset, remembering the average wage is £5 (US$10, DM15) a week, and give him at least double. It's still cheap by European standards.

STREET BEGGING

The outright beggars of The Gambia are the children, and you should resist all temptations to give them money. We can acknowledge that the self-appointed guide is a beggar in disguise, but the only other people who will accost you for money in the streets are a few paralysed young men in wheelchairs around Bakau, who carry sponsorship forms and ask you to sign your name and write the amount you give. What you do is a matter for your own conscience.

Toubab. A toubab is a white person. The word is understood in all the tribal languages in much of west Africa, inferring that it is borrowed from another language. Some people argue it came from the English 'two bob' (two shillings, now 10p), as the amount of a tip or a day's wage, but this is highly unlikely as the most common European language of the region is French.

7: THE PERSONAL TOUCH

My Gambia

THE GAMBIANS ARE A FRIENDLY PEOPLE, even more so up-country away from the disturbing influence of the tourist hotels and European affluence. I was making my first journey to Georgetown in a minibus from Serekunda when a fellow-passenger started a conversation with me. What was I doing? Writing a guide book? Excellent! He gave me many snippets of background information which have found their way into these pages, then he suggested I should see the Police Commissioner at Soma, where our ways were to part.

"Why? Do I need police authority to go inland?"

"Not at all. But you will find the police chief can open so many doors for you. It will be well worth your while, you will see."

Gradually, as our journey proceeded, I realised my companion was something more than the average Gambian. He was full of vitality and he greeted almost every new passenger as a friend, speaking to them — he told me — in any of several tribal languages. Finally I had to ask him. "Everybody seems to know you: should I? I'm sorry, but I don't."

"Alhaji Hassan Njie," he said. "Alhaji means I've been on a pilgrimage to Mecca, and Njie —" he pronounced it *inyay* "— is the family name. I'm a presenter on Radio Gambia and I'm on my way to a remote village to do an interview. When you're back in Banjul give me a ring and we'll arrange an interview for you, if you have no objections."

I hadn't. And I was impressed to see the way the police at the tiny post at Soma greeted this celebrity in their midst. Hassan Njie told them that Mr Palmer wished to see the Commissioner for a letter of introduction, then he went to arrange transport for the remainder of his journey.

The chief of the Soma police apologised to me because the Commissioner was not in the village but in 'Masa Konk' about three kilometers away. It was unseemly that I should be forced to go by taxi, so we waited awhile until the post's new Land-Rover answered a radio appeal to take me to the Commissioner in the administrative village of Mansa Konko.

The constable behind the wheel was suitably impressed with his errand but pointed out that he could not ask the Commissioner for a letter of introduction for me unless he first had a letter to introduce himself to the Commissioner.

As soon as the constable had his authority we drove off, and he was pleased to show me the Land-Rover's refinements, including its flashing blue light. We turned off the tarmac road and drove along a dirt track to Mansa Konko, pulling up outside the police station. My constable hurried inside with his own letter and soon a sergeant emerged to tell me, with regret, that the Commissioner was not in the village. Would I be able to accept his deputy?

"Certainly. Perhaps you can help me yourself; I don't want to waste anybody's time." I told him exactly what my mission was.

"No, sir. It is not a waste of time; it is what we are here to do. I will escort you to the deputy."

The deputy lived in a large European-style bungalow rather than a traditional African compound, and as I was ushered in I noted the large television set in the corner and the smart furniture and carpet. An enormous black man in a white kaftan stood in the centre of the room with a smaller man lying at his feet. I offered the big man my hand but he declined it, and the smaller man spoke.

"Mr Palmer. I am so sorry to greet you in this position but I am suffering from an attack of malaria. I have a terrible headache."

I knelt beside him and explained my mission, apologising once more if I seemed to be wasting his time; as the big man silently left the room I realised he was a passing friend. The deputy commissioner listened to my story then wrote in my notebook:

To whom it may concern: I, Mr S. L. Jonko, Deputy of Police, officer commanding 'B' Division Mansa Konko, hereby declare that I have had the honour of speaking to Mr Palmer who explained to me that he is researching a guide book for tourists on The Gambia. Should any concerned body or person assist him in these regards it would be considered with much gratitude.

Thank you, Mr Jonko — and Mr Njie. The letter proved very useful and instantly opened a number of doors for me. And on the day before I left The Gambia I went to the studios of Radio Gambia and recorded an interview with Edmund Thomas for the 'People, Places, Ideas' programme.

On the buses. I reached Georgetown at my third attempt. With my letter of introduction in my pocket I left Soma in a bush taxi destined for Georgetown, but the driver decided to go to Basse Santa Su first; as that was the next village on this itinerary I decided to leave the taxi there. My second attempt to reach Georgetown also failed, and on my third try I caught a GPTC bus from the main depot at Banjul.

"This bus goes to Georgetown?" I asked somebody in the little wooden GPTC office nearby.

"Yes. Not all the way. It stops at the ferry and you must walk across MacCarthy Island."

We reached Soma uneventfully, passed the police station where I had begun my Land-Rover journey to Mansa Konko, and pulled into the big bus depot on the east of town, scarcely disturbing the vultures who strutted around the diesel pump as if waiting to be refuelled. The passengers for Soma and the nearby smaller villages clambered out, leaving maybe 30 for the onward journey.

A few moments later the driver moved his bus across the depot, manoeuvring it with meticulous care close beside another bus already standing there, with its doors open and maybe a dozen people inside. When he had effectively barricaded that other bus's doors with his own vehicle, trapping its passengers inside, our driver switched off his engine and turned to us with a statement in one of the local languages.

Instantly there was a mad rush for the exit, and a young man spared a few seconds to tell me in English "This bus goes no further. That is the Georgetown bus," and he pointed to the vehicle alongside us.

One or two slender people managed to squeeze between the coaches and into the newly-designated Georgetown bus, but others, realising they had no hope of following, remounted the vehicle they had just left and made the perilous transit through two sets of windows.

I stood in the depot and watched in anger as old men and buxom women squeezed into that other bus, and I realised that with a rucksack and a case full of cameras I would not be able to follow. Once again Georgetown had eluded me, even though I had a ticket to the place.

I walked back into Soma and found a bush taxi. "Georgetown?"

"Yes, white man."

"And Basse?"

"And Basse. Georgetown first, Basse second."

I had heard *that* story before, but I was determined to make it to this elusive Georgetown even if I had to travel via Fatoto. But I was almost the last passenger for the bush taxi and within minutes we were on the road. As we passed the GPTC depot I noticed the two buses were as I had left them; I found some little satisfaction in knowing that the Georgetown bus never passed us on the road and I reached Macarthy Island quicker than I would have done had I managed to squeeze myself and my luggage out through one coach's window and in through another's.

Bus timetable. I had earlier asked the Director of Tourism if he had a copy of the Gambia Public Transport Corporation's timetable for the country, and he had directed me towards the GPTC head office and depot at Kanifing. After that incident at Soma, which was amusing in retrospect, I decided to visit the Kanifing depot on my way back to Banjul.

I met several of the senior staff, and they were all considerate when I

The baobab tree has large seed-pods containing tartaric acid. These trees are at Bintang beside the Bintang Bolong.

explained my problem. I wanted a copy of the timetable not only for myself but to put in this book.

"But — we don't have a timetable! There is no need! Everybody knows what times and routes our buses travel!"

"I don't," I pointed out.

They promised to work something out for me, and when I called back a few days later Mr Tamba Samba, the schedules officer, was drafting the corporation's first timetable. "It's my job to know where the buses and their drivers stay overnight, and where they go the next day," he explained. "I carry all that information in my head, and so does each driver. And the passengers learn by experience what the schedules are. However..."

He began with the first driver of the day to leave Banjul. "He goes at 0642, and it takes him four and a half hours to reach Soma, then another four and a half to Basse, so..."

Within the hour we had the rudiments of our timetable. It is, as Mr Samba stressed, subject to the hazards of the route: passenger problems, police checks, punctures, bad roads. And, I add from personal experience, bus drivers with strange parking habits.

DISCOVER THE GAMBIA

8: THE PACKAGE HOLIDAY

The Tourists' Gambia

THE GAMBIA'S TOURIST HOTELS offer a wide range of accommodation and activities, catering for almost every taste. The smartest and most expensive is the Kairaba, which opened at the start of the 1990-91 season.

The largest is the Senegambia, closely followed by the Palma Rima; the smallest is Fransisco's, followed by Sambou's and the Romana. The quietest is probably the Wadner Beach, and the cheapest is the Friendship, a gift from the Chinese government and, frankly, in the wrong place for a tourist hotel.

All the tourist hotels, and some of those in the indigenous market, have been obliged to charge a 10% tourist tax since November 1988 in place of the the flat-rate tax that applied until then, but the tariffs quoted in the following chapter are for casual visitors and are not necessarily the rates paid by the package tourist who has the advantage of block bookings. Prices include the 10% tax, and breakfast, unless otherwise shown, and the list is alphabetic.

AFRICAN VILLAGE

Location: Atlantic Boulevard, Bakau; **Address:** PO Box 604, Banjul; ☎95034, 95307, 95384; telex 2239 AFRODEV GV.

Tariff. Sgl from D300; seaview dbl room D600; season Oct-May.

The African Village is an easy-going hotel with the original accommodation in straw-roofed African-style huts. The one-acre site is close to the centre of Bakau with the CFAO supermarket, banks, and night clubs only a few minutes' walk away. The main part of the

The African Village Hotel has The Gambia's only island bar.

hotel is on level ground but the gardens slope, with some terracing, to the 20-ft (6m) cliff, and access to the beach down a path and steps.

Background. The hotel, which earns a three-star rating in operators' brochures, was built as a night club, the 'Club 98,' by the Milky family from Lebanon who are prominent traders in The Gambia: you will see the name Milky in Russell Street, Banjul. The night-club became a 28-bed hotel in 1974-5 as tourism increased, with accommodation as now in individual huts; in the 1975-6 season the number of beds was increased to 43. Fire badly damaged the hotel in 1978, and in 1979 it was rebuilt, including 17 huts with bath, bidet and balcony, 22 huts with shower, and 34 smaller huts without either. There is no longer any connection with the Tropic Gardens Hotel, also built by the Milky faily.

Accommodation. Further expansion and extension has increased the accommodation to 160 beds in 80 huts, every one with either a bath or shower and all at ground level.

Restaurant. The clifftop Seaview Restaurant also overlooks the beach and serves breakfast, lunch and dinner; there's an à la carte restaurant and beach bar.

Activities. Activities include a weekly discothèque, video films, and frequent African dancing. There is table-tennis, darts, a conference room, and two cycle-hire firms operate on the main road near the gate.

The pool is advertised as the only one in The Gambia to have an island bar, its beauty enhanced by coconut palms leaning out over the water.

Tour operators. Gambia Experience, Redwing, Vingresor.

AMDALAYE VILLAGE HOTEL

The Amdalaye is under construction by Kololi Beach, and promises to be the country's top-ranking tourist hotel. Its owner, Mohammed Kebbe, already owns the Amdalaye Bus Company, the Amdalaye Trading Enterprise, the Great Alliance Insurance Company, and Caira Publishing Co.

The Amdalaye Hotel is to have 24 self-catering three-bed bungalows fitted out to the highest European or North American standard, including dishwashers, integral garages, and satellite television receiving CNN (Cable Network News) from the USA.

AMIE'S BEACH HOTEL

Location: On Cape Point, beside Cape Point Bungalow; **Address:** PO Box 600, Banjul (shared with Palm Grove Hotel); ☎95035, 95106.

Tariff. Rate varies, but double around D550. Year-round season.

Background. Opened by President Jawara in November 1988, the Amie's Beach is owned by Gambian businessman S.S.Ceesay, who took three years to build it and then named it from his wife; Mr Ceesay is also the owner of the Palm Grove, one of the country's original hotels.

Services. The gardens are centred on the pool, the biggest in The Gambia until outstripped by the Palma Rima's. The hotel's three bars and three restaurants are named from Mr Ceesay's sons, Babu's Bar being the main poolside watering hole while Musu's Disco, open from 2100 to 0400 or later, features live entertainment.

There's a good range of beach sports, including windsurfing, and the hotel has its own professional tennis coach. The management claims the hotel's supermarket is probably the best in the country, and there are two boutiques.

Accommodation. You'll find 120 rooms, all with twin beds, and 48 self-catering one-bedroom apartments sleeping up to four people who must be on good terms.

Tour Operators. Cosmos, Gambia Experience, Enterprise, Hetzel, Airtours, Sunworld.

ATLANTIC HOTEL

Location: Marine Parade, Banjul; **Address:** PO Box 296; ☎28601-6; UK reservations, 0800 (free call) 414741; **Telex:** GV 2251.

Tariff. From £65 per person; year round season. All credit cards accepted.

The Gambian-owned Amie's Beach Hotel had the country's largest pool for only a few months.

The Atlantic Hotel in Banjul is the country's meeting-place, either in the lounge or here by the pool.

Background. The original Atlantic Hotel was built in 1953 on the opposite side of Marine Parade; the typical colonial- style structure with green-painted corrugated iron is now used as government offices.

The 'new' Atlantic, designed by a Mexican called Louis von Waberer, built by Balfour Beatty, and given a four-star rating by tour operators, lived up to its claim of being The Gambia's leading hotel until outrated by the Kairaba in 1990. It opened for business in 1979 but had an official opening on 11 December 1980 by President Jawara.

Whatever you want of any hotel, The Atlantic can supply. It is the automatic meeting-place in The Gambia, much as the New Stanley Hotel in Nairobi, with its famous thorn tree, is the rendezvous in Kenya. It acts as an unofficial agency for several local tour operators, and it's where you can make contact with Mass Cham the bird man.

The Atlantic is in the Copthorne Hotels group, based at Horley, Surrey, which is now part of the Aer Lingus Group following its buy-out of the British Caledonian Group's hotel interests. Tourist taxis wait by the front door, where there is a list of priced destinations ranging from the Abuko Nature Reserve to Cap Skirring in Senegal. Closer, a two-minute walk takes you to the beach or the National Assembly, and a ten-minute walk brings you to MacCarthy Square.

Accommodation. The three-storey white building with a gently curving façade, has 200 double rooms and four suites, all with bath and shower and most with air conditioning. The design is pleasing and enhanced by coconut palms at the front.

Restaurants. The Dunda – 'High Life' – an à la carte restaurant, seats 120; the Bantaba coffee shop seats 200; and there are smaller beachside and poolside snack bars. (A *bantaba* is a group discussion by the village elders.)

Activities. The Atlantic offers a wide range of sports from aerobics to volleyball: take your pick from jogging, squash, tennis, bowls, crazy golf, darts, sailing, waterskiing, and paragliding. Three Tesito – 'Togetherness' – rooms are available singly or in multiples to provide conference facilities for 100 or for 450 people. The hotel also offers telex and secretarial services for the businessman who takes his work on holiday.

Tour Operators. Gambia Experience, Hayes & Jarvis, Kuoni, Thomson, Wings, Cosmos.

BADALA PARK

Location: On approach road to Kotu village. **Address:** PMB 467 Serekunda, ☎90400-1, fax 90402.

Tariff. High season, dbl D575; year-round season.

Background. Owned and developed by Gambian Abdoulie Mboge, this smart hotel opened in November 1991. There is a hint of Moroccan influence in the architecture, with grounds extending towards the mouth of the Kotu stream and the beach. The gardens were begun during building work, so they are well established.

Services. There is a good Sunbird à la carte restaurant, and entertainment is provided; the hotel has 100 rooms and 20 suites.

Tour Operators. Enterprise (Owners Abroad), Spies, Sunworld, Hayes & Jarvis, Airtours.

BAKOTU

Location: 100 yards from Kotu Beach with access through the *bengdula* (tourist market); **Address:** PO Box 532 Banjul; ☎95555.

Tariff. Sgl from £25; season Nov-April

Background. The hotel is beside the golf course but *ba kotu* means 'near the creek,' and it is indeed close to the little stream called the Kotu which gives its name to the area. The Bakotu, given a two-star rating by operators, is one of the smallest of The Gambia's tourist hotels and has an intimate atmosphere; built in 1976 by a Swedish-Danish consortium, and opened for business in 1977, it was extended in 1979 and again in 1991. The design of the conventional buildings is welcoming and at split-level, with a strong Scandinavian influence. A children's pool and play area complement the main pool; some sports added in 1981.

Accommodation. 98 chalets offering 196 beds.

The Badala Park Hotel is one of the latest on the tourist market.

Restaurant. The hotel has its own buffet and the restaurant is run by a contractor. Beyond the hotel, the Kotu Beach area has several independent restaurants and night clubs.

Cycle hire is available outside the gate, where there is also a bank, a telephone box for international calls, a craft market that stages drum music and lively tribal dancing well into the night, and a large tourist taxi depot.

Tour Operators. Horizon, Thomson, Tjaereborg, Jet Reisen.

BANTABA

Location: On the main Senegambia to Fajara road. The hotel is being built as I write; the architecture is impressive, but the hotel is on the *wrong* side of the road, involving a 10-minute walk to the beach.

BOUCARABOU

Location: Between Kololi and Bijilo villages (see map of Bakau & Serekunda area) ten minutes' walk from beach; **Address:** PO Box 2491 Serekunda; ☎812048-9.

Tariff. Sgl D240, dbl D380; weekly D1,500, D2,200. Season, mid-October to end of May, but may extend into July.

Background. The Boucarabou is off the beaten track and caters for people looking for seclusion or cultural experiences, particularly

The Bakotu Hotel has a strong Scandinavian atmosphere.

African music. The hotel has 'drum and dance' classes lasting three weeks, and 'water music' excursions on the river; *boucarabou* is the Jola word for a ceremonial drum.

The hotel was financed by 14 German and one British investor, and believes in conservation: it has its own well, and uses solar energy backed up by a generator, and there's an excellent vegetable garden.

Accommodation. Thirteen double rooms, with more to come.

Tour operator. Cool Running Tours, Eisenacherstr 71, 1 Berlin 62, bringing clients from Germany, Austria and Switzerland; others can book themselves in.

The German-owned Boucarabou Hotel caters for lovers of music and culture.

BUNGALOW BEACH

Location: In Kotu Beach, at the head of the tarmac road from the west, beside the tourist market and fronting onto the beach, its front gate 30m from the Bakotu Hotel; **Address:** PO Box 2637 Serekunda; ☎95288, 95623; Telex: 2318, Fax 96180.

Tariff. Sgl £48, dbl £65, high season; open all year.

Background. Built in 1973 by the Scandinavian consortium responsible for the Bakotu and the Kotu Strand and financed from Sweden.

this is one of the few self-catering tourist hotels in The Gambia, and is open all year.

The grounds have well-tended lawns, which is unusual in this climate, with a scattering of coconut palms, hibiscus and bougainvillea. The wall which separates the grounds from the public beach is only thigh high, but the hotel has daytime security patrols.

Accommodation. The Bungalow Beach is a neat but unpretentious mini-village of chalets in two-storey blocks under corrugated-iron roofs, its name often abbreviated to 'BB.' Chalets are of identical design except that those on the first-floor have balconies; in each, the kitchenette has a cooker and fridge (the hotel has its own generator), and one of the two couches in the dining area opens to provide a third bed if required; the main bedroom is at the rear, with the shower room and wardrobe leading off.

Restaurant. Continental breakfast with fresh bread is delivered to each chalet, and there is a bar, an à la carte restaurant, and a mini-supermarket for those self-catering meals. The hotel also has its own hair salon. Sir William Bar and Restaurant is nearby on one side, with the tourist market on the other, and five minutes along the beach takes you to other bars.

Cycle hire is available outside the gate, where there is also a bank, a telephone box for international calls, a craft market that stages drum music and lively tribal dancing well into the night, and a large tourist taxi depot.

Tour Operators. Gambia Experience, Spies, Imholz.

The Bungalow Beach Hotel has self-catering two-storey chalets as an option.

CAPE POINT BUNGALOW

Location and address: At Cape Point, Bakau, beside the Sunwing Hotel which occupies the tip of the peninsula; ☎95005.

Tariff. Dbl, D290; apartment D390. Nov-April season.

This is one of the smaller tourist hotels; built in the mid-1980s it had 14 rooms in bungalows but was extended to 18 rooms for the 1988-89 and to 29 for the 1990-91 season. The bungalows are of conventional block construction with corrugated iron roofs set in well-tended grounds with an abundance of coconut palms and other tropical trees, and access to the splendid beach. There are two restaurants, one of which has an à la carte menu.

Tour operator. Vingresor.

Bananas add a touch of charm to the Cape Point Hotel.

FAJARA

Location: At the extreme west end of the tarmac road which begins as Atlanic Ave in Bakau; a footpath extends past the golf course to connect with the tarmac road by the Bungalow Beach Hotel; **Address:** PO Box 2489 Serekunda; ☎95351

Father Jara gave his name to the village of Fajara, and so to the Fajara Hotel.

Tariff. Sgl D450. dbl D550, triple D650; year-round season.

Background. Opened in 1971, the hotel changed ownership several times in its first years but has now become an established part of the tourist circuit. It is a collection of buildings occupying a sloping site of 1.5 acres running down to the beach, and with a tall security fence all around. It's a hotel for family holidays, granted a two- or three-star rating by operators.

The reception hall is large and airy with a welcoming red carpet and a large wall-tapestry of The Gambia. It opens onto a partly-covered terrace with a splendid view of the grounds, the beach, and some spectacular sunsets over the Atlantic Ocean.

Entertainment. There is a giant chess set in the grounds, with African characters instead of the more conventional kings and pawns; sports include pool, table tennis and crazy golf, with the main golf course only a 'drive' away. The Fajara Casino Club offers roulette, blackjack, poker, and the usual range of slot machines. There is also a conference centre.

The hotel, owned by Basiru Jawara who also controls the Wadner Beach, is on a five-year lease to a German-Greek consortium.

Accommodation. There are 93 double rooms with balcony and en-suite bath, in a three-storey block, 172 double bungalows and a few singles, giving a total of 512 beds.

Tour operators. Spies, Thomson.

FRANSISCO'S

Location. In the Fajara beach area. **Address:** PO Box 2609, Serekunda, ☎95332.

Tariff. Dbl 450. Year-round season.

Background. Fransisco's began as a bar-restaurant and broke into the hotel market in the season of 1988-89. It is the smallest of the tourist hotels with just eight rooms, but it is by that very reason one of the most intimate and has earned a three-star rating with operators. The gardens are a real showpiece, containing hundreds of species of tropical plants and representing years of collecting.

Run by Britons Stuart and Joyce who bought it from its Danish owners, Fransisco's is set amid luxurious vegetation and is still renowned for its restaurant. Each room has two or three beds, fridge, and air-conditioning. No pool or entertainment, but they're nearby; so is the beach.

Tour Operator. Gambia Experience.

Stuart, joint-owner of Fransisco's Hotel, leaves the bar.

FRIENDSHIP HOTEL

Location: Mile 7, by the football stadium at Bakau, a mile from the beach; ☎95829-31.

Tariff (bed and breakfast): sgl D160, dbl 195, year-round.

Background. Begun in 1980 and completed in 1983 as a gift from the Chinese government to accommodate sports people in the neighbouring stadium, the Friendship was first called a 'hostel' but changed its name to 'hotel' for the 1988-89 season. It definitely is *not* a hostel, but its unusual location puts it out of the market for tourists who must have the beach at their doorstep.

The Friendship is a smart if slightly austere four-storey L-shaped building with a formal garden and a tennis court; there is no pool. Conference facilities are available and visitors can opt for room only, bed and breakfast, or full board.

Accommodation. Seventy-eight double rooms. This is the cheapest of the tourist hotels and if you're on a budget but looking for comfort you could take a flight-only deal and book yourself in here - but remember the stadium and the long walk to the beach.

Tour Operators. None, but some operators use it for sporting occasions.

HOLIDAY BEACH CLUB-HOTEL
This hotel is being built near the Kololi Beach Club.

The Friendship Hotel was a gift from the Chinese Government, but it's some way from the beach.

The Kairaba is The Gambia's only five-star hotel. The hotel catering school, seen here, sets the standards.

KAIRABA

Location: Between the Kololi Beach Club and the Senegambia Hotel; **Address:** P.M.B. 390, Serekunda; ☎92940-2; fax 92947, telex 2283 KAIRABA GV.

Tariff. Standard room, dbl from £85, studio £105, premium suite £150; presidential suite (sleeping six) around £250.

Background. The Kairaba opened in May 1990 as the most luxurious, best-equipped, and therefore the most expensive hotel in The Gambia, with a five-star rating, and within weeks it hosted the 13th Ecowas summit and the Liberian peace talks. The main buildings include a conference hall seating 800, with a hotel training school nearby, sitting in 15 acres (60,000sq m) of landscaped grounds fronting onto the beach.

The hotel is owned by Gamnor, a consortium headed by a Norwegian with a 52% share, and including the Gambia National Investment Board, the German Development Society (Deutsche Entwicklungsgesellschaft), and a Dutch financier. Gamnor also owns the close neighbour, the Senegambia Hotel, which shares with the Kairaba a generator producing 2.1 megawatts, equal to a quarter of The Gambia's public electricity supply. The Kairaba has 200 staff, mostly African, while the Senegambia has 500. The anticipation is that

45% of visitors will be British, 15% German, and a furter 15% Swiss and French; the management speaks English, French and German.

Accommodation. Take your choice from 74 standard rooms, 19 de luxe, 20 studios, two premium suites and the presidential suite, arranged in 12 blocks in the beautiful tropical gardens which spill over from the Senegambia and are home to many exotic birds – and the occasional monitor lizard.

Restaurants. The Kingfisher and Malimbe, with the Monsoon bar and the Bolong bar.

Other services. Day and night room service, laundry, baby-sitting, hairdresser, and on-site **Hertz car rental** in association with the Senegambia Hotel.

Entertainment. None – but guests are welcome to use the Senegambia's extensive entertainments, q.v.

Tour operators. Gambia Experience, Hetzel, Jet-Reisen, Kreutzer, Neckermann, Redwing, Select, Sindbad, Transair, Trident Travel (Austria), TUI.

KOLOLI BEACH CLUB

Location: South-west of the Senegambia, making it the furthest from Banjul, ☎96313, 94897. **Mortgagors for intending buyers:** Philip Smith, ☎0803.314803 (Torquay).

Background. This enterprise began life as a club, with 'clubshare' apartments, a variation of timeshare without the hard sell, marketing itself as 'The Gambia's five-star co-ownership haven,' a title which it still claims, but in the 1988-89 season the Kololi Beach Club entered

Most visitors to the Kololi Beach Club have bought clubshare membership, but non-members are also welcome.

the package hotel business in a small way, earning a four-star rating in the Serenity brochure. The club intends to keep this side of the business small, but it has expanded slightly.

The one- and two-bed apartments, be they for club members or private rental, have been equipped and furnished to the highest European standard, and are now marketed as self-catering bungalows; they have *tiled* roofs and are undoubtedly the smartest and most up-market self-catering premises in The Gambia, with a daily maid service and fully-equipped kitchens with microwave ovens, but under-occupancy supplements make them more economical for parties of four to six people.

Services. The site of necessity has its own shop, and there is a boutique, pizzeria and pool, plus evening entertainments.

Tour Operators. Cosmos.

KOMBO BEACH (NOVOTEL)

Location: Kotu Beach, between the Kotu Strand Hotel and the tourist market, and facing the Bakotu; **Address:** PO Box 694, Banjul. ☎95465-8; telex 2216 NOVO GV; **Reservations:** USA, ☎(212).499.0734 (NY); (213).649.2121 (CA); Germany, ☎611.742598.

Tariff. Sgl £66, dbl 78, suite £102; year-round season.

Background. Built in 1981 for the Caledonian Hotel group, it was opened in 1983 under its present owners, the large French Novotel chain, and is confusingly known either as the Kombo Beach Hotel or the Novotel.

Open all the year, it has a four-star rating from British tour operators who supply 90% of its visitors, with the remainder coming from Germany, Scandinavia, France and the United States.

Entertainment. The Kombo Beach is one of the liveliest hotels in The Gambia with giant chess, water polo, two pools, two tennis courts, windsurfing, archery and the use of a cycle, all free, plus possible temporary membership of the Fajara Golf Club for a fee of £8.

Evening entertainment includes discos, the Bellengo night club, live African music (the hotel's staff provides the entertainment twice a week), theme evenings with African dancing and folklore, live music, video shows (some at a fee), and floodlit tennis. The grounds have well-kept lawns.

You will also find an on-site shop, laundry, telex and telefax, clinic, a baby-sitting service and daytime entertainment for the children to allow parents some freedom, and there's a 300-seat conference room.

Cycle hire is available outside the gate, where there is also a bank, a telephone box for international calls, a craft market that stages drum music and lively tribal dancing well into the night, and a large tourist taxi depot.

Accommodation. The hotel has 250 air-conditioned rooms and eight junior suites, holding 516 beds and set in four three- storey blocks located in a tropical garden. All rooms have bath, telephone, radio, balcony or terrace, and room service. The poolside bars have African thatch roofs.

Restaurants. The restaurants are the Lekukai, the Kudula poolside restaurant, and the à la carte Rive Gauche with French cuisine; there are bars in the lounge, at the poolside, and in the Kudula restaurant.

Tour operators. Africa Tours, Gambia Experience, Hayes & Jarvis, Hetzel, Hotel Plan, Jet Reisen, Kreutzer, Kuoni, Neckerman, Sovereign, Thomson, Uniclam, Horizon.

The Novotel, also called the Kombo Beach, is one of The Gambia's liveliest.

KOTU STRAND VILLAGE

Location: Beside the Kombo Beach (Novotel) at Kotu Beach; **Address:** PO Box 957 Banjul; ☎95609.

Tariff. High season sgl D450, dbl D550; year-round season.

Background. Designed and built in 1979 by the Scandinavian team responsible for the Bungalow Beach and the Bakotu, the hotel changed owners in November 1987. It is a quiet and small place in

The Kotu Strand offers intimacy, with splendid bird-watching potential just beyond the gate.

distinct contrast to its neighbour the Kombo Beach, with an easy-going and relaxing atmosphere. The reception desk and the entrance overlook the Kotu creek and its mangroves, while the grounds have coconut palms, bananas, pawpaws, hibiscus and tamarisk — and lawn that came as turf from the Bungalow Beach: lawns are almost as unnatural in west Africa as pawpaws are in Europe.

The hotel is popular with bird-watchers because of its setting, between the Kotu Creek and the beach. I've seen quite a bit of bird life in the area as well as a four-foot (1.3m) monitor lizard, quite harmless.

Services. The bar-and-reception has 24-hour service, while the main bar-restaurant has a good à la carte menu catering for diabetics and vegetarians on request. The large pine-furnished lounge leads to the beach bar, supermarket, boutique, and the pool with its sun terrace.

Entertainment. Table tennis, darts, African dancing and acrobatics, ballet and fashion shows.

Cycle hire is available outside the gate, where there is also a bank, a telephone box for international calls, a craft market that stages drum music and lively tribal dancing well into the night, and a large tourist taxi depot.

Accommodation. There are 30 double rooms each with shower and fridge, and two two-storey blocks with 16 self-catering apartments and 12 double rooms.

Tour operators. Hetzel, Intasun, Lancaster, Neckermann, Spies, TUI.

The largest pool in The Gambia is at the Palma Rima.

PALMA RIMA

Location: Access from the main tarmac road from Fajara to the Senegambia; **Address:** P.M.B. 350, Serekunda; ☎93380-1, telex 2360 PALMRIM GV; fax 93382.

Tariff. Sgl D660; year-round season.

Background. The hotel opened for business on 1 October 1989 with large octagonal bungalows each holding several apartments, all on the ground floor. The extensive grounds, with their original kola palms but without exotic gardens, front onto the beach.

Entertainment. The hotel claims to have The Gambia's largest pool, taking the title from Amie's Beach after less than a year. The 130-seat Moonlight Nightclub has a large dance-floor with special-effect lighting, and the 400-seat theatre offers tribal dancing, cabaret, or films. And there's a conference and banqueting hall.

Accommodation. There are 152 double rooms, all with fridge and some with air-conditioning.

Tour Operators. Cosmos, Gambia Experience, Airtours, Thomson, Spies, Enterprise, Sunworld.

PALM GROVE

Location: On Cape Road between Banjul and Denton Bridge; **Address:** PO Box 600 Banjul; ☎28630, 28632-3; telex, 2213 PALMHOT GV.

The Palm Grove offers peace and quiet, between the bustle of Banjul and Bakau.

Background. One of the original hotels of The Gambia, the Palm Grove opened in 1968 when there were less than 1,000 visitors a year to the country and Bakau was a small African-style village. The hotel's original owner was Scandinavian Air Systems – the SAS airline – and in those early days the Palm Grove had 10 rooms; the Milky family bought it in 1975 and three years later extended it to 54 double rooms plus 14 suites, but it has recently been bought by Mr S.S. Ceesay who also owns the new Amie's Beach Hotel, and it's now back under European management, and refurbished in 1992.

It's a quiet and intimate hotel with a good beach and within reasonable access of Banjul, two miles away; if there's no tourist taxi waiting outside, the bus stop is a short walk away with the fare into Banjul a mere D2 The National Holiday Service coaches, running the airport shuttle and special excursions, are based here.

Accommodation. The reception area was rebuilt and extended in 1982; a conference room followed, and more guest rooms, bringing the total to 110 rooms, providing some of the most spacious accommodation available in The Gambia.

The theme is peace and quiet, with no disco and no noisy water sports and, although the nation's principal road runs past the gate, now a superb four-lane dual carriageway, and a large peanut processing factory is on the horizon, peace and quiet have not been violated.

The hotel has a very large pool and immediate access to an

undisturbed beach, but there is now a growing threat from coastal erosion.

Restaurant. Furnished in local bamboo, the restaurant offers a good selection of international cuisine and Gambian dishes.

Tour Operators. Enterprise, Hayes & Jarvis.

ROMANA HOTEL

Location: Atlantic Boulevard, Bakau; **Address:** PO Box 2500 Serekunda; ☎95127.

Tariff. Sgl D275; year-round season.

Background. The Romana opened in May 1988 with 11 double rooms and in its first year it relied on word-of-mouth recommendation, casual callers, and the taxi drivers. It's obviously small and intimate, and its bar-restaurant opens onto a small but well-stocked garden and neat lawn.

The manager and chef is Swiss-born Henry Fröhlich who has a good reputation back home and is adding to it in The Gambia; the restaurant is open to non-guests: see 'Restaurants.'

The hotel was badly damaged by fire in 1990, after which its Swiss owner sold to Gambian Aladge Secko, who reopened in 1992.

Tour Operator. None; had been listed by The Gambia Experience.

The Safari Inn has only nine rooms, but its restaurant has seating for more.

SAFARI INN

Location: At the eastern end of the tarmac road from the Senegambia, near Kairaba Ave; ☎95887.

Background. The Safari Inn opened in 1989 with nine double rooms, and a 22-cover bar and restaurant open daily 0700-2100 catering for a middle-range clientèle. All rooms have en-suite shower, with a double tariff of £18.

Tour Operator. None; was listed by The Gambia Experience.

The roof of the Senegambia Hotel's reception area is a masterpiece.

SAMBOU'S HOTEL

Sambou's Restaurant on Old Cape Road entered the package holiday market in 1986 as Sambou's Hotel, contracting its five double and five single rooms exclusively to Vings. If there's a vacancy it costs D200 single, D350 double; ☎95237.

SAVOY HOTEL

Location: Opposite the Palma Rima, q.v.

The Savoy Hotel was planned to open in 1991 – but this is Africa!

The Senegambia is large, lively, and has acres of floral gardens.

Clubhotel SENEGAMBIA BEACH

Location: On Kololi Point, at the end of the tarmac road from Banjul;
Address; PO Box 2373 Serekunda; ☎92717-9; telex, 2269 SGBH GV;
fax, 91839.

Background. The largest hotel in The Gambia, it stands in 20 acres
(8ha) of landscaped grounds that retain as many of the original
coconut palms as possible; native plants added after the contractors
left are all labelled in English.

Built in 1982, it opened at the end of that year as part of the Gamnor
group, hinting at Norwegian finance; see the Kairaba.

The Senegambia's main reception hall is one of The Gambia's
architectural masterpieces, corrugated iron roof an' all, which with the
large site makes this a hotel you are not likely to forget.

Accommodation. There are 305 rooms and 10 suites, plus studios
with kitchenettes for long-stay visitors as the hotel is open all the year.
Accommodation is either in the main building or in one of several two-
storey blocks, the first-floor rooms having balconies; they are all built
to a rectangular design and have corrugated iron roofs.

Entertainment. Nightly folklore or cabaret shows are held on the
specially-designed stage, and available sports include pool; squash;
tennis on four courts, some floodlit; table tennis; mini golf; two
volleyball courts; two pools and two paddle pools; archery, billiards
and darts. There are bars at the beach, the pool and the terrace, and
a main bar which doubles as a disco.

A Hertz car rental agency is on the premises, available also to guests at the adjacent Kairaba.

Restaurants. You have a choice of four restaurants; the à la carte Flamingo, the Table d'Hôte, the Coffeeshop- Pizzeria, and the Terrace: the coffee shop with the Asian Food Corner is open until 0100.

The hotel, given a four-star rating by operators, accepts only American Express among the plastic currencies. There are special rates for groups, diplomats, companies, long-stay guests, and for visitors in the summer rainy season.

My wife is standing by Sait Matty Bah's tomb in the grounds of the Sunwing Hotel.

Tour Operators. Gambia Experience, Cosmos, Hayes & Jarvis, Hetzel, Columbus, Jet Reisen, Kreutzer Touristik, Nur Tourisuc, Musair, Sovereign, Owners Abroad, TUI, Aviatours, Jetair, Tjaereborg, Aviareisen, Club Viaggi.

SUNWING

Location: At Cape Point, Bakau, with the sea on two sides; **Address:** PO Box 2638 Serekunda; ☎95428; telex 2220 SW GV.

Tariff. Mostly package; base is D440 for individual bookings.

Background. The Sunwing was the idea of the Swedish tour operator Vingresor and the SAS airline, but was designed by the Briton Peter Gibbons and now has a Spanish manager. It opened in 1971 and was overhauled in 1979, giving it a four-star rating.

The grounds merge with the beaches on each side, and probably give you the best opportunity in The Gambia of seeing coconut palms overhanging the golden sands, the image that so many people have of the tropics. As the hotel is on a headland where currents can be noticeable, the beach has a lifeguard and lookout tower, and swimming is not allowed from the tip of Cape Point.

Tomb. The lush vegetation in the eight acres of grounds includes pomegranates, pawpaws, more coconut palms similar to those which line the hotel's approaches, and baobabs, which like to send their roots beneath sea level; in the front garden there is also the tomb of the imam (holy man) Sait Matty Bah, whose name has been given to a road in Fajara.

Accommodation. The Sunwing can accommodate 400 guests in 200 rooms, each with en-suite shower.

Restaurants. Breakfast and dinner are served buffet- style in the pizzeria, but there is an à la carte restaurant and a beach terrace snack bar.

Entertainment. Activities include watersports around the pool, table tennis, volleyball, crazy golf and — mainly for the Scandinavians — an early morning keep-fit class.

Tour Operators. Thomson, TUI, Vingresor, Gambia Experience, Airtours, Jetair.

TROPIC GARDEN

Location: On Atlantic Boulevard, Bakau, near the African Village Hotel; **Address:** PO Box 2576 Serekunda; ☎95369; telex 2272.

Tariff. Sgl D350, dbl D450.

Background. Built in 1975 by the Milky family of Banjul to be run as a nightclub — the Club 80 — it became the Tropic Bungalows Hotel and eventually took its present name. It was completely overhauled in 1986 and now warrants a three-star rating in operators' brochures.

The site is a compact 2.5 acres (1ha) sloping down to the 20-foot (6m) cliffs overlooking Bakau beach; access is by all-weather wooden stairs unofficially shared by the visitors at the adjacent Atlantic Guest House.

The Tropic Gardens is convenient for the activities that Bakau has to offer; a branch of the Standard Chartered Bank at the gate, the Avis car agency nearby, and at the road junction the CFAO supermarket, another bank, the Gamtel office, police, bush taxis and tourist taxis.

Accommodation. Single-storey African-style huts hold 57 double rooms and 13 suites.

Restaurants. The main bar and restaurant has a nautical theme, with 21 lampshades made from the dried skins of puffer-fish, and with four sea-water aquaria holding turtles, rays and multi-coloured sea-horses from local waters. There's also an à la carte restaurant and bar, a wine bar, and the so-called Horses Pop snack bar.

Entertainment. Entertainment includes the Topaz Night Club, live African music, and games centred around the pool. There are two pools; the children's pool is less than three feet deep. Come with 49 other people and you can hold a conference here.

Tour operators. Cosmos, Intasun, Pool 90 (Italian), Vingresor.

WADNER BEACH

Location: On Cape Road, near Denton Bridge and to the west of the Palm Grove Hotel; **Address:** PO Box 377 Banjul; ☎28199; telex 2219 WADNER GV.

Background. The Wadner Beach is a self-proclaimed hedonist's delight for that perfect laid-back holiday. Built in 1971 by Mrs Brit Wadner of Sweden who had earlier established Radio Syd, the hotel later came into Gambian ownership and subsequently fell from grace. It was closed for the 1986-'87 season and refurbishment restricted its use in '87-'88, but it reopened in October 1988.

The Tropic Gardens Hotel has rondavel-type accommodation at the poolside.

The location of this and the nearby Palm Grove (q.v.) determines the hotel's guest list and therefore its character. It is 2.5 miles (4km) from Banjul whether you travel by GPTC bus, tourist taxi, or hire one of the Wadner Beach's cycles, and Bakau and its amenities are three miles in the other direction, so the hotel concentrates on promoting its excellent beach, absolutely empty to the west but now facing the problem of erosion, and its relaxed evening entertainment: videos, discos, and a weekly African evening. Guests can also play pool, table tennis, or use the large swimming pool.

The Wadner Beach has scope for watersports, but the beach is eroding.

Accommodation. There are 250 double rooms.
Restaurants. A main restaurant, and one with an à la carte menu.
Tour operators. Gambia Experience, Thomson.

SAFARI CAMPS

Safari camps are not tourist hotels. They are of traditional African *rondavel* design – the circular mud-hut with a thatched roof – but they have a selection of several European refinements such as plastered walls, a ceiling, en-suite toilet, electricity – although seldom do they have them all. There is some loss of comfort, usually compensated by the sense of adventure, of 'going native.' All are on the itinerary of the ground operators' excursions – or they should be.

LAMIN LODGE

Just two miles from the airport, this lodge is a bar and restaurant built on stilts thrust into the bed of the Lamin Creek; it's 20 minutes' walk from the main road. The restaurant opens at 0700 for birdwatchers, and for other clients at 0800, closing at 2000. The lodge is a stopping point on some organised excursions, and in turn it organises its own, such as pirogue trips to Denton Bridge or Banjul, or sleeping in the pirogue *Jamond* which holds 15 people.

The lodge is run by the man who originally ran Jangjangbure, which is now in his wife's management. Address: PO Box 664, Banjul; phone enquiries, ☎95526, but the phone is not at the camp.

BONDALI CAMP

A tourist camp is under construction at Bondali Jola, south of the Bintang Bolong, on the site of a Bainunke warrior camp of bygone centuries; the grave of the Bainunke marabout is claimed to be nearby. Bondali has nine *rondavels* (circular, thatched huts) and a conventional toilet block, and was opened in April 1992, but later that year it closed for alterations.

TENDABA CAMP

The name means 'large wharf,' *tenda ba,* so the stress should be on the 'ten,' not the 'da.' This camp is 62 miles from Banjul and three miles from Kwinella on the main road. There is no address as there's no postal delivery, no phone, and water is from the camp's wells, pumped up by the generator which supplies the electricity.

Take as much water as you can carry or you'll be reduced to sampling the 100 brands of whisky which the Swedish owners, Willi and Anders Karlsson, claim to have in the bar.

Tendaba opened for business in 1972 and has a capacity for more than 100 people but is virtually never fully-booked, so the independent traveller unable to phone for a reservation can afford to risk that hike from the main road.

The Gamtours 'Bush and Beach Safari' at Tanji

A laterite road crosses a marsh on the way to Bintang

Fatoto ferry is one of the most picturesque settings in The Gambia

On a Black and White safari

Accommodation. Visitors sleep in rondavels, typical African grass-roofed huts, with twin or double beds; family huts take four people who will be on good terms by the morning even if they weren't the previous evening. The suites by the river bank are permanently reserved for government officials and some expatriates.

Excursions. Tendaba organises its own excursions as well as being on the itinerary of other firms' safaris. The morning or evening two-hour creek cruise by pirogue takes visitors to the bolongs on the northern shore and plunges into the dense mangrove; for £5 this is an unforgettable experience for people who spend their working lives with feet under a city desk. A two-hour Land-Rover safari into the bush shows nature in the raw and usually gives an insight into the vast amount of bird life in west Africa.

The RAF operated an airstrip here at Tendaba in the Second World War; it's still viable and has been used on rare occasions by light aircraft such as the Africana Air machine you might have seen at Yundum. Nowadays the clearing provides an alternative habitat for birds — see the checklist in 'Wildlife in The Gambia' — and the miniature zoo stocks nothing but crocodiles.

Food. Tendaba is a wonderful place for eating: if you're going up-country independently, make the most of it for from here on your only European meals will be at Eddie's Hotel in Farafenni and Jangjangbure Camp on the north bank, and at the new Jem Hotel and possibly the Linguere Motel, both at Basse on the south bank.

The 'large wharf' – Tendaba – flies the Swedish and the Gambian flags.

Sofanyama Camp has a wonderfully picturesque setting.

A typical Tendaba breakfast is a Scandinavian-style smörgasbord, but the faint-hearted can opt for the à la carte menu. Lunch is straight from the river, usually kingfish or ladyfish, and dinner is nearly always warthog, unless you opt out for religious reasons. Wild warthog may not sound a delectable dish but it's pleasant; there's no flavour of pork and the meat resembles the darker flesh of the turkey.

A reader recommends Tendaba's cold giant prawns, called shrimps on the menu, eaten with plenty of bread and a garlic dip.

The **tariff** is payable in any currency, as long as it equals £8 per person per night, and £5 for dinner.

KEMOTO CAMP

The most isolated of safari camps in the most remote of Gambian villages, Kemoto Camp is at the village of the same name at Mootah Point, where the river makes a sharp bend south of Kerewan. It's 20 miles along laterite roads from Sankandi on the main tarmac highway, but much more accessible by boat. The camp is Spanish-owned and opened late in 1992 with a pool and around 20 huts.

SOFANYAMA CAMP

Don't be put off by the fact that this camp's name in Fula means 'drink your own urine,' but you may be deterred by its condition:

Gamtours stopped using it in 1992 until its standards were improved. When I realised the loose-weave low-hung ceilings in the huts could hold the prospect of unlimited surprises in the night, I decided I'd rather sleep in the open. There's no pump, either, so all water, for drinking and showers, is hauled from the well. And there's no generator. The tariff for any of the 11 double rooms in the four huts is D140.

The camp, owned by the chief of Jarra East district, is sited on the flood plain of the Sofanyama Bolong by Pakali Ba, making it unusable in the rainy season; it was washed away in the summer of 1988 during construction. The location, and the camp, are picturesque, and 187 species of birds have been seen here, as well as hyaenas, wild dogs, aardvark and mongooses.

Griots, the wise men who keep tribal history alive by telling it to the children, claim that ages ago a large crocodile lived here, killing men and cattle until a Brikama trader named Bamba Bojang slaughtered it. The ruins of Bojang's settlement survive on a hill to the east of Pakali Ba, near some doum palms, now rare in The Gambia. The doum is distinctive as the only palm to have branches.

JANGJANGBURE CAMP

German-born Peter Losen and Gambian Ebon Jange started Jangjangbure (pronounded ~*burry*) in 1988, but Peter has quit,

Jangjangbure Camp has an exotic riverside setting north of George-town.

leaving his wife here while he looks after Lamin Lodge. This idyllic setting on the north bank of the Gambia River, east of Lamin Koto and opposite Georgetown on MacCarthy Island – Janjangbure Island – is the furthest point reached by coach on any organised excursion, and is a useful stopover for the Wassu circles.

The camp has 48 beds, most in seven communal rooms but with six singles and two doubles; most rooms have access to toilet and tap, with water pumped from the camp's own well – but there's no electricity: lighting is by hurricane lamp. Breakfast is from 0700, usually to the exotic sound of the laughing dove and the bulbul's call of 'quick, doctor, quick,' and the fruit bats are on the wing as you dine in the tropic night. Troupes of green vervet and red patas monkeys live beside the camp.

The tariff is D110 per person, plus optional meals. Address and phone as for Lamin Lodge.

RIVER CRUISES

Jangjangbure has its own excursions, notably aboard the *Jamond* back to Lamin Lodge, carrying 40 passengers by day or 15 overnight – or by the converted tugboat *Hans* upstream towards Basse. At the time of writing, these are the only upper-river cruises available in The Gambia. The Atlantic Guest House operates the *Sea Empress,* a 7-metre 5-passenger motor boat in the Oyster Creek area.

The *Spirit of Galicia,* a British yacht which operated cruises for Kuoni and others, ceased trading in 1992, and the *St Mawes Castle,* which began life as the St Mawes to Falmouth ferry, has never proved itself on the Gambia River.

You are therefore missing the chance to see the islands in the river, although Fort James Island is still accessible on organised excursion.

Islands. Elephant Island is named from the pachyderm which has not been seen wild in The Gambia since the 1900s. The creek which separates **Pappa Island** from the south shore is a breeding area for hippos and crocodiles, and you may perhaps see some of these creatures if you take the ferry from Jarreng to Carol's Wharf. The **Baboon Islands** are a 1,448-acre (586ha) national park, designated in 1968 and closed to the public. And the head of navigation of the Gambia River is the **Barrakunda Falls,** just over the border in Senegal.

EXCURSIONS

Around 30% of package tourists buy an excursion and so see something of the real country. Organised excursions are priced at a level which the market will bear, and they offer comfort, although their clients see The Gambia from a privileged position. Several tours take people to areas they would not visit by any other means, but you could duplicate some trips at a fraction of the price although probably taking twice the time.

GUIDED TOURS FOR BIRDWATCHERS – Mass Cham

Mass Cham is the country's leading ornithologist, who represented The Gambia at a pan-African bird conference in Burundi in 1992. His tours are:

Mon: Bund Rd area, Banjul, 1600-1800hrs.

Tues: Bird safari, 0600-1200.

Thurs: Atlantic Hotel bird show, from 1830.

Fri-Sun: Bird tour to Barrakunda Falls, driving to Jangjangbure and by boat to the falls, for £120.

Contact: home, ☎28043; personal callers, 64 O.A.U. Blv (Leman St) Banjul; post, c/o Atlantic Hotel, PO Box 296, Banjul; fax 27861.

The following excursions are advertised in the tourist hotels. Some may not be available for the season, and all are subject to a minimum number of passengers booking. For **more informal** excursions organised by smaller concerns, see 'Land-Rover hire' under 'car hire' **or** contact Montrose Holidays, Bijilo, PO Box 2436 Serekunda, fax 90023, or leave a message at the Senegambia Gamtel office.

CREEKS – Gamtours, West African Tours, Sunshine Holiday Tours.

There's no difference between a creek and a bolong, but this excursion organised by Gamtours is usually sold as the 'Creeks Tour.' A coach takes you to Denton Bridge where you board a vessel which the tour operators call a 'pirogue,' a sea-going fishing vessel of the type the Portuguese introduced to west Africa in the 15th century.

This all-day trip takes you first to Lamin where you may be able to gather oysters from the mangrove roots, and then to Mandinari where your adventures continue with an ox-cart ride into the village or a cruise around the smaller creeks in a 'pirogue' — this time it's a dugout canoe with extra timbers added to make the sides: don't stand up in a hurry!

ROOTS – Gamtours, Sunshine Holidays.

A comfortable cabin cruiser takes you on this all-day excursion from Banjul first to **Fort James Island** which the English captured in 1661 and used as a holding station for freshly-caught slaves awaiting shipment to the New World. The fort is named from the king who was to become James II.

Albreda. The cruiser berths at Albreda on the north shore, where stone-built slave houses still stand on the river bank, with steps leading down to the water's edge rather like Traitors' Gate in the Tower of

The Gamtel office is on the site of this old open-top well in Soma (above); Mass Cham fills his flask from the new street tap that replaced the well.

London, except that this was the last footstep on African soil for hundreds of thousands of negroes destined for slavery. A rusting cannon, reminiscent of colonial wars between England and France rather than of slaving campaigns, still points its muzzle out towards the river.

Juffure. From Albreda a ten-minute walk takes you to Juffure, probably the best-known village in west Africa after Alex Haley discovered that his great-great-great-great-grandfather Kunta Kinte had been born in this area and taken from the slave house still standing here, to labour in the United States. Recent research concludes that of the 8,500,000 to 11,000,000 slaves taken from Africa, no more than 500,000 went to North America.

BUSH and BEACH SAFARI – West African Tours, Sunshine Holiday Tours.

This excursion takes you through the bush in suitable vehicles, the drivers having a loose itinerary which allows them to turn aside in search of wildlife, but they also call at specific villages to see palm sap being tapped to make 'jungle juice:' see *Discover Tunisia* for more on palm wine.

The second part of the journey is memorable as the trucks hit the coast at Solifor Point and drive back along the beach. At certain phases of the moon the beach drive comes first.

TENDABA CAMP – West African Tours, Gamtours.

A two-day safari by road to the camp, meals and accommodation included in the price but you pay extra if you sample all those whiskies.

Tendaba's own excursions. While here you have the option of sampling the camp's own expeditions, either exploring the bolongs by outboard-powered pirogue, or going into the bush by Land-Rover.

In the evening you'll probably watch more dancing which, in the best African tradition, involves lively acrobatics and contortions to the staccato beat of the drum. You may be invited into the bush before dawn to see and hear the new day beginning.

AFRICAN EXPERIENCE – West African Tours, Sunshine Holiday Tours, Gamtours.

An evening trip through the Kombos – Bakau to Gunjor – with a wide variety of cultural entertainment and a chance to sample Gambian cuisine cooked and served in a Gambian compound; you may be invited to lend a hand. You will start the evening with a glass of palm wine and gradually progress to a rather potent Gambian punch – drink as much as you want, as you've already paid for it.

FOREST AWAKENING – Gamtours, West African Tours, Sunshine Holiday Tours.

This is one for all birdwatchers, with a maximum number of 12 per party. You're collected by an off-the-road vehicle before dawn and driven to Tanji near Solifor Point for daybreak. Now on foot, a European ornithologist takes you around local habitats ranging from mudflats and beach to savannah and mangrove swamp, and helps identify the many species you'll see. After breakfast, back to the hotels by midday.

ABUKO and BRIKAMA – Gamtours, West African Tours, Sunshine Holiday Tours.

An early morning to mid-afternoon excursion visiting The Gambia's only nature reserve open to the public (the Baboon Islands National Park is closed to visitors), followed by a look at the woodcarvers in the craft market at Brikama.

WRESTLING – Gamtours, West African Tours.

Wrestling is immensely popular with Gambians, and the singing, dancing, drumming and whistling sideshows make it an entertaining sport for Europeans, even without the contests in the arena. The organised expedition takes you to Serekunda on a Saturday or Sunday, except during Ramadan.

There is nothing to prevent you going to a wrestling match on your own. If you choose a location near the coastal villages the fee will be at least D10 – less if you're black – but up-country it's a standard D5, or less.

LAND-ROVER SAFARI (SOUTH GAMBIA ADVENTURE) – Gamtours, West African Tours, Sunshine Holiday Tours, Black & White Enterprises.

A 90-mile (145km) tour in an open Land-Rover through the bush and along dirt tracks into South Gambia (the Kombos, down to Gunjur), with a visit to a development project to which you contribute D5 in your ticket. Some areas are strict Moslem, so no naked thighs and no video cameras. You might see baboons and monkeys.

CITY TOUR – Gamtours, Sunshine Holidays.

A full day, starting with a visit to Serekunda market, the liveliest in The Gambia, plus the batik workshop in Bakau, followed by a tour of Banjul, probably including a visit to the museum and (when it's rebuilt) the colourful Albert Market on Wellington St.

CHAMPAGNE and CAVIAR CRUISE – Gamtours, Sunshine Holiday Tours.

This excursion is particularly vulnerable to the availability of suitable boats. If it's operating, you leave Denton Bridge for a day afloat in a large pirogue, cruising Oyster Creek and the other bolongs behind Banjul, then out into the river where you may see the school of resident dolphins. Champagne buffet, and afternoon tea.

KAFOUNTINE – Gamtours, West African Tours.

Kafountine is the nearest coastal village in southern Senegal, and this day trip takes you, via a brief look at the Brikama craft market, through Séléti to Kafountine. After a day on the beach, you make a detour on the return journey to see some tribal dancing.

TWO-or THREE-DAY SAFARI – Gamtours, West African Tours, Sunshine Holiday Tours, Black & White Enterprises.

There is a choice of destination as well as operator. Two days can take you by road to Jangjangbure Camp and Georgetown; or to Dakar and its environs; or to Ziguinchor and the Casamance. The former offers reasonable overnight accommodation; the second gives you the experience of a safari camp; the third involves a night in basic quarters deep in Senegal. If this is your only taste of adventure you will find it a distinct contrast to the luxury of the tourist hotels – but this is the *real* Africa.

One safari visits Ziguinchor, the capital of the Casamance, and you spend the night in a basic camp deep in the teak forest: there are showers and toilets, but no electricity. On the second day you visit the unusual two-storey mud houses of Mlomp, with the chance to go by

Wrestling is the national sport, but football is a close second.

dugout canoe on the Casamance River as an optional extra.

Bring as much drinking water as you can, but don't bring video cameras. This excursion is real adventure and is not suitable for children, and if you need a visa the operators will arrange for it, which means they need to hold your passport from Thursday morning until departure on Saturday. The visa fee is extra.

SEVEN-DAY TOUR OF CASAMANCE AND NYOKOLO KOBO NATIONAL PARK – West African Tours, Gamtours.

Great adventure, but for around £350 it's a lot of money in addition to the tourist hotel bed you're *not* sleeping in.

FISHING SAFARIS

The main ground operators offer a range of fishing trips, usually around the estuary or in the creeks behind Denton Bridge.

CONTACTS

Gamtours: ☎92259, 92505; PO Box 101, Banjul.

Black & White Enterprises: ☎93174, 93306; PO Box 201, Banjul.

Sunshine Holiday Tours: ☎93236, 93478; PO Box 493, Banjul. All three companies are based in the Kanifing Industrial Estate.

West African Tours: ☎95258.

GAMBIAN HERITAGE SAFARIS

Gambian Heritage begins operation with the 1993 winter season, working with the new ground operator **Eco Tours,** established in January 1993 with experienced staff from Gamtours, and with a wide range of vehicles. Gambian Heritage is headed in Britain by Terry Palmer, and Dennis Hawes who has operated holidays in Britain for US visitors; Mass Cham is the company's ornithologist in The Gambia.

The company's policy is to open up the country, and nearby parts of Senegal, to European visitors, with a range of around six or seven excursions, starting with a two-week **Gambian Adventure Safari** exclusive to Gambian Heritage. This safari is designed for people who don't normally used organised travel, and it includes a couple of nights sleeping in native compounds in rural villages, possibly a night under canvas, several river trips otherwise unobtainable, and it is the first 'organised' safari to use accommodation upstream of Georgetown. It includes a visit to Bansang Hospital and almost all the country's places of interest. It is truly adventure – but with the sting taken out.

As interest increases in the Gambian hinterland, and the necessary infrastructure slowly grows to cater for it – except for the highway to Soma – this safari represents the best way to see the country with some degree of comfort, and to meet the people in their own environment.

At the other extreme, the two-week **Senegambia Birds** expedition around The Gambia and into the Tambacounda or the Nyokolo Kobo area, offers a considerable degree of luxury. **Birds of The Gambia** is a two-week exploration mostly confined to The Gambia, but both tours take in much more than birds and also show travellers the country's culture and history.

Some holidays, such as **Beach and Basse,** spend a week around the coast and a week inland, and there are three one-week holidays which can be taken separately, or in any combination, or with a second week doing whatever you please. The coastal-based weeks give you the options of taking excursions based on sightseeing, on meeting the people, or on birdwatching; the river trip uses craft not normally available outside the charter market.

Informality. Gambian Heritage's policy is to aim for informality: the company does not normally use any of the hotels in the package holiday market, preferring places such as the Bakadaji Bungalows and the Kololi Tavern, Tendaba Camp, and the Gem Hotel in Basse. Parties are intentionally kept small, with an absolute maximum of 20 people, usually travelling in two vehicles.

Other accommodation. Gambian Heritage also acts as booking agent for many – but not all – of the non-package accommodations listed in the next chapter.

Contact. For further details contact the publishers, Heritage House, at 5 King's Road, Clacton-on-Sea, CO15 1BG.

This child at Albreda has yet to learn of the tragedy of the slave trade. Her 'roots' are safe in The Gambia.

ROOTS OVERLAND – West African Tours.

Take the ferry to Barra and go by road to Juffure and Albreda, looking in at the Berending sacred crocodile pit.

RIVER GAMBIA NATIONAL PARK ADVENTURE – West African Tours, Sunshine Holidays.

By road to Georgetown and on to Peter's Place (Janjangbure Camp) for lunch. Afternoon at the Wassu stone circles. Next day, a five-hour river trip ending at Sapu, opposite the Kai Hai Islands, and bus back to Bakau. You might see hippos and crocodiles.

AFRICAN CULTURAL WORKSHOPS – Sunshine Holidays.

A choice of trying your skills either at pottery, African cooking, batik, tie-and-dye, or dancing to the beat of African drums.

FIVE-DAY BIRDWATCHING – Sunshine Holidays.

A trip for the birdwatching enthusiast, with night stops at Tendaba and Jangjangbure. The third day takes you to Nyokolo Kobo National Park in south-east Senegal, a vast tract of unspoiled terrain holding the headwaters of the Gambia River in impressive hill country. Return to Tendaba for the last night.

CULTURAL SENEGAL – Black & White Enterprises.

An adventure safari into deepest Senegal, where *toubabs* are rare and life is primitive. You see how the people of the Casamance live, visit a teak forest, see the two-storey mud houses of Mlomp, and take a pirogue trip. Overnight stay is basic, and children are not accepted for this safari.

BACKGROUND TO THE EXCURSIONS

GAMTOURS

Gamtours is really The Gambia National Tours Co Ltd, carrying the motto 'for development of tourism in The Gambia.' The Gambia Public Transport Corporation owns 99% of the shares and the government the remaining one percent, putting Gamtours into the private sector of the economy.

Gamtours is by far the largest provider of organised excursions, using staff and vehicles specifically for the purpose. Where tours call at villages in need of basic supplies the company makes a point of distributing visitors' gifts to the needy and to the local schools.

Operations manager Mrs Farma Njie told me: "Medicines are also much-needed items and the Royal Victoria Hospital in Banjul will definitely appreciate them. Visitors can bring along clothing and other assorted items for destitute children; there is an SOS children's village here which will appreciate such gifts."

SUNSHINE HOLIDAY TOURS

Sunshine Holidays is a newcomer to the market, with Farma Njie moving from Gamtours to become the director of operations here. "The company has a fleet of Mercedes coaches, six of them in the luxury class," she said. "At the start we handled Spies, Uniclam and Pool 90, but we have plans for moving into the British and German side of the market."

BLACK AND WHITE ENTERPRISES

The company took its name from its founders, John Saunders and Aziz Khan, but is now totally Gambian. It started by renting Land-Rovers with drivers, and had two cars for self-drive hire, but B&W has now moved on to a fleet of 15 Land-Rovers, all for hire with driver, either on an organised excursion as listed above, or for charter by a party for a tailor-made safari.

ALEX HALEY and *ROOTS*

You can scarcely visit The Gambia without hearing about the slave trade and the black American Alex Haley who traced his family ancestry back to Juffure, on the north bank of the Gambia River.

A bush taxi loads up in Basse. There may be 500kg on the roof and 15 people inside – but the cow must walk.

Roots, the title of his book as well as of the Gamtours excursion to Juffure, is the story of Kunta Kinte, a boy of the Mandinka tribe who was snatched early one morning as he went to chop wood after spending the night on the lookout for slave raiders. The grandson of a marabout (Islamic holy man), Kunta was landed in America at 'Naplis' and sold to a plantation owner. He escaped four times and had half his foot chopped off to prevent a fifth attempt.

After gradually accepting his fate, Kunta married Bell who had a daughter Kizzy late in life. Kizzy was brought up as the massa's daughter's plaything, but when she showed a streak of independence at the age of 16 she was sold, never to see her parents again. Raped by her new massa, Tom Lea, Kizzy gave birth to Chicken George, who eventually managed to gain his freedom in his declining years.

The book gives a powerful insight into conditions on the American plantations in the 18th century, in which each generation of this family impresses upon the next the story of that original African Kunta, who came from 'Kamby Bolongo.'

Chicken George's eighth child, Tom Murray (slaves took their current massa's surname) married Irene, and their seventh child Cynthia became Mrs Will Palmer, wife of a respected black businessman in the United States, and grandfather of Alex Haley.

Haley managed to piece together the parts of his vast jigsaw, passed down through six generations, and with the clue of 'Kamby Bolongo' suggesting the Gambia bolong, he came over to visit the country. Eventually, with help from the *Readers Digest*, he met a griot, a man whose mission in life is to remember tribal and family history and to teach it to his eldest son; the griot told him in Mandingo of Kunta Kinte, who went to chop wood and was taken 'about the time the king's soldiers came.'

Haley pursued his detective work in London and the United States, establishing that in 1767 Colonel O'Hare's forces — the 'king's soldiers' — came from London to guard Fort James. And on 5 July 1767, the *Lord Ligonier* under Captain Thomas Davies sailed from the Gambia River for Annapolis — 'Naplis' — clearing the customs on arrival on 29 September, 1767.

On 1 October, Haley established, the *Maryland Gazette* advertised the sale on 7 October of 'a cargo of choice healthy slaves.' The ship had left Africa with 140 unwilling passengers, including some women and children, but only 98 had survived the crossing and were to be, at auction, probably more valuable than the remainder of the cargo of beeswax, ivory, cotton...and a trace of Gambian gold.

EATING OUT

The Gambia's traditional dishes rely heavily on groundnuts, rice, fish and chicken, the staples of life, boiled or fried over an open fire.

Relatively few Gambian menus have been adapted to the kitchens of the tourist hotels or of the Banjul and Bakau restaurants, but among the dishes you should try are **benachin** or variations of this spelling, and also known as **jollof rice,** a rice-based stew with various meats, tomatoes and other vegetables, depending upon what's available. Jollof, by the way, is just one of 20 ways of spelling the name of the Wollof tribe.

Peanut puré is the main ingredient in **domada,** which also has rice and meats, and of **tio grio,** which is a peanut soup with very little added.

The Mandinka word for 'chicken' is *sisay*, with **sisay yassa** being chicken marinated in onion and garlic, with pepper, vinegar and lime juice added for further flavour; **sisay nyebi** has peas and beans, and **sisay bassi** is chicken with millet, both with added flavourings and spices. You can then work out that **base nyebi** has peas and beans, this time garnishing a beef stew.

Fish. The river and the ocean provide plenty of fish, which the Gambians have traditionally dried as they lacked other means of preserving the harvest. With the coming of refrigeration, fish is gaining popularity on the hotels' menus, and you will find barracuda hiding under the bland name of sea pike, and catfish going by its tribal name of njunga. Tilapia – Nile perch – makes a tasty dish, as do mullet, the near-boneless butter fish and the delicate flesh of the ladyfish, all of which taste so much better if barbecued in aluminium foil with a hint of tomato or peanut puré. Smoked bonga fish makes a

The fish-smoking sheds at Tanji produce some tasty bonga.

splendid snack, the flesh dropping easily from the bones; you can get plenty of bonga in the Tanji fish-smoking sheds for less than D1 each.

For several seasons The Gambia has been loading excellent shrimps and a few lobsters into the cargo holds of planes returning to Europe. You'll also find them on the menu in local restaurants, along with oysters from Oyster Creek, which are tasty and perfectly safe when smoked.

Fruit. As The Gambia is in the tropics, it produces a wide array of delicious fruits. You will see pawpaws growing on tallish stems in your hotel grounds, and those enormous trees with deep-green leaves that you see throughout the country, produce mangoes in spring. There are bananas in plenty, though the fruits are often shorter than we find in Europe; there are avocadoes, pomegranates, passion fruit, aubergines, water melons and a very few locally-grown pineapples.

Drink. The fashionable drink, a Gambian alternative to the cocktail party, was Earl Grey Green Tea, but this has given way in certain quarters to 'jungle juice,' the sap of the palm tree which has been allowed to ferment naturally, so making it highly potent. You may see a few trees with clusters of bottles tied just beneath the crown of leaves.

This menu is a compilation from the Romana Restaurant and Sambou's Bar, upper-middle-range establishments, to give an idea of prices, which are subject to change:

> Ladyfish, boiled, with potatoes & parsley sauce D40
> Barracuda, fried D40
> Fish au gratin D42
> Scampi with sauce piquante D38
> Omelette, natural D33
> Terrine de volaille au poivre vert D42
> Filets de sole marinés D38
> Jambon de Parma 'Romana' D48
> Coeur de filet de boeuf D90

RECIPIES

Here's a recipe for Wollof rice, for which I thank Rosemary Long of Montrose Holidays:

To a cupful of groundnut or palm oil in a pan, add an onion, a garlic clove, and two cupfuls of whatever is available from ocra, cassava or pumpkin, all chopped. Soften the vegetables in the oil, then stir in 3 cupfuls of dry rice; stir until the rice is cooked in the oil, then add water as needed. Also add a touch of tomato puré and a stock cube.

And Rosemary's version of fish and chips, African style, which is *not* a traditional dish:

Spread ground nut oil on aluminium foil, add sliced onion and

The jetty at Bintang dominates the waterfront

The new Great Mosque in Banjul is truly great

The laterite road to Fatoto is wide and has a good surface, but it's dusty

Main street, Soma

potatoes and the prepared fish; pour on a small amount of tomato puré mixed with water, crumble two stock cubes, add a crushed garlic clove, heaped teaspoon chili powder, and more oil. Top with a bay leaf. Wrap the foil and cook on a barbecue.

BARS and RESTAURANTS

Outside the tourist hotels, which obviously have their own restaurants, the scope for eating out in Banjul, Bakau, Fajara and Serekunda is small, but is increasing year by year. Eating out in The Gambia is more expensive than in a restaurant of comparable quality in the UK, despite the lower costs.

This is an attempt at the impossible task of listing *every bar* (♈) *and restaurant* (✗) *in the country* of interest to Europeans, the result of much legwork, and help from several people.

The list is alphabetical.

Abbi's, Palma Rima; German take-away.

African Heritage Gallery & Restaurant, 16 Wellington St, ☎26906. Daily, 1000-1600, this first-floor balcony ✗ is popular with expatriates. Access easy to miss; roughly opposite the Shell garage. Splendid view across the estuary, excellent art gallery and shop, the best WC in Banjul – and good food as well.

Al Basha, beside Senegambia Hotel, Lebanese menus; ☎93300.

Ali Baba, a small Indian ✗ on Atlantic Ave, opposite Tropic Gardens.

Ambassador Bar & Restaurant, on Kairaba Ave, Serekunda. A smart, German-managed ✗ with an excellent beer cellar.

Athina, 41 Kairaba Avenue, ☎92638. Opened 1992 as 'the ultimate in elegance and fine dining,' serving Greek and Lebanese dishes 1830-2400 daily.

Baalbeck, at 78 Atlantic Ave, Bakau, near the Tropic Gardens, ☎96120. It opened in 1989 offering an international cuisine; 1800-2400 except Mon.

Bakadaji Bar & Restaurant, Badala Park Way, Kotu Point, 100m from Palma Rima. Gambian and European dishes, served in pleasant surroundings. Opened October 1989, middle-class; 300 covers. ☎92307.

Bamba Dinka, on corner by CFAO, Bakau, with a garden setting. Mon-Sat 1500-0100, Sun 1700-0100.

Bamboo, near the Kotu Beach complex, ☎95764, daily 1700-2300. Chinese dishes.

Big Bite, Kololi Beach; a McDonalds-style take-away.

Bistro, Kairaba Ave, Serekunda, ☎92638. Formerly the Lamar, with a Lebanese cuisine.

Bobo, on Sait Matty Rd, near the stadium. Opened Dec 1988; owners Jan and Mike travelled overland from UK and now claim 'the prettiest English-run ♉ in The Gambia.' 1700-200 or so. ex Sat.

Bobo, on Albion Place, Banjul. Same owners as above; opened 1990 to catch trade from 1100 to 1430 Mon-Sat. 34 covers in air-conditioned comfort.

Braustüble, top of O.A.U Blv (Leman St), Banjul. Dine inside or in the secluded gardens. Popular with tour organisers but no air-conditioning.

Cape Point, Bakau; European and Gambian menus; ♉ opens 1000-2400; ☎ 95005.

Cedar Club, Kairaba Ave, Serekunda. Lebanese menus.

Chez Henri, near Badala Park Hotel, Swiss-owned.

Churchill, opposite the defunct casino; British-owned; daytime snacks, evening meals, ☎90830.

Clay Oven, Cape Point; smart Indian ✕.

Dam's Place, Kairaba Avenue, middle-range ✕ with European dishes, Gambian-owned.

Di' Vino, Lebanese-owned wine ♉ and ✕ near Senegambia Hotel; 1800-0200, ☎ 90600.

Dolphin Bar, beside Kairaba Hotel, access from hotel car park, 0900-2400 ex Mon; British-owned pub and ✕.

Eddie's, Farafenni. See chaper 9.

Follonko, rest-house, ♉ and ✕; European and Gambian menu. In Kartung, South Gambia, close to beach.

The Paradise Beach bar is one of many places for your beachside drinks.

Fransisco's, in the Fajara complex, ☎95332. Has moved into the tourist hotel business, q.v., but is still an excellent ✗, with exotic gardens.

Galaxy Bar & Restaurant, Kairaba Ave, Serekunda. Also has a few rooms to let.

Golden Dragon, 75 Kairaba Ave, Chinese menus.

Hand in Hand, Bakau; quiet British-style pub.

Il Mondo's, behind the Bungalow Beach Hotel; British owned, open 0900-2300.

Jamaa Bar & Restaurant, 59 Leman St, Banjul. Opened in 1988. Gambian and European cuisine.

Jangjangbure Camp, north of Georgetown; see earlier this chapter.

Jem Hotel, English-run hotel and restaurant due in Basse by 1994.

The Jungle, a ⚲-✗ off Mamakoto Rd, Bakau, south of the petrol station; open 0700 daily. Owner Fred Knottage was featured in *The People* for marrying too often.

Klaus, Bakau; a McDonalds-style take-away.

Kololi Tavern, Kololi; smart African-style hotel with ⚲-✗ in the garden or under the trees. ☎93410. No music, and no late nights.

Kotu Bendula Bar & Restaurant, between the Kombo Beach and Bungalow Beach hotels. Gambian and European dishes; African dancing each evening. ☎95219. Daily, from 0930.

Lamin Lodge, Lamin; see earlier this chapter.

Latina, 27 Kairaba Ave, Gambian-owned, specialising in steaks, fish and pizzas; 0900-2400 daily, ☎92249.

Leybato, Danish-owned beach ⚲ at top of Kairaba Ave by the water tank.

Lotus Restaurant, Kairaba Ave, Fajara. Formerly Le Saigon, but still with Vietnamese and Chinese meals. Daily, 1700-2300.

Madeleine's Inn, 17 Kairaba Ave, ☎91464. Restaurant and take-away started in business December 1990, daily 0800-2400 or so. Swiss and international cuisine.

Marie's Pub, a small British-style ⚲ on Old Cape Rd, open 1500-0300 or so. Run by Swede Kurt Graap and his Gambian wife, who claim it Gambia's 'favourite pub.' ☎95037. All drinks, and some sandwiches.

Mermaid, Kololi Beach area.

Oasis Night Club & Restaurant, 2 Clarkson St, Banjul, ☎26996. Daily 0000-0200; the place to meet Senegalese beauties.

Palma Nova Bar, on Kairaba Ave, Fajara; smart, and with a good menu.

Paradise Beach Bar, smart ⚲-✗ running beside the beach; on path between Bungalow Beach and Fajara hotels. Closed at sunset.

Paradise Inn, beside Kololi Tavern, British-owned ✗ in motel.

Poco Loco, Cape Point Rd, Bakau, British-owned and run since March 1992; daily 1100-0200. Café-🍸; ☎96719.

Rainbow Restaurant, by the Kairaba Hotel. Open daily 1200-2400, with Gambian and European cuisine. Medium to high class, no live music.

Romana, Atlantic Ave, Bakau, near CFAO; ☎95127. Opened in May 1988 as a 🍴 and small hotel under Swiss management. Middle- to upper-class, but gutted by fire August 1990; now back in business.

Rude Boy, Swedish 🍸 in Bakau new town.

Safari Inn, Fajara, near Fajara Hotel. Middle-class 🍸-🍴, opened 1989 with 22 covers; daily, 0700-2100. ☎95887. Is also a small tourist hotel, q.v.

Sahib, Kombo Beach; Indian 🍴 specialing in herb dishes.

Sambou's, Old Cape Rd, Bakau, ☎95237. Reasonable prices for good quality. The place is also a tiny tourist hotel, q.v. Quiet.

Scala Restaurant & Night Club, on the western approaches to Kotu complex. Up-market, Danish-style 🍴, with night club. ☎90813.

Serendip, 105 Kairaba Ave, ☎95760; Sri Lankan meals from 1200-1500, 1800-2300; ☎95760.

Siam Garden, Fajara, 1700-2300, Thai dishes; 1700-2300, ☎96141.

Sir William, a smart German-owned 🍸-🍴 beside the Bakotu Hotel, lively in evening; ☎96111.

Solid, a 🍸-🍴 and night club at the north end of Kairaba Ave, Fajara.

Solomon's Bar, on Kololi beach by the old casino and the coming Amdalaye Hotel. Recommended by the *Sunday Times* and as a result Yorkshireman John Bodie went into partnership with Solomon Barry and rebuilt the 🍸. The partnership has dissolved.

Steak House Garden Restaurant, Kololi Beach area, with international cuisine daily from 0630; see Taj Mahal.

Sunu Bar, Atlantic Ave, Bakau; Swedish and Gambian owned, open to 2100.

Taj Mahal, one of several associated businesses opened 1992; this is near the Kairaba Hotel and serves Indian cuisine daily from 0630. PO Box 2772 Serekunda, ☎93309, fax 92709.

Tendaba Camp, see earlier in this chapter.

Tin Pan Louie's, Fish and chips on Kairaba Avenue.

Tropic Smiles, 42 Atlantic Ave, Bakau. Seafood and meat specialities. Mid price range. Daily 1100 until late.

Uncle Joe's, Nelson Mandela St (Cameron St) Banjul, a 🍸 in what was Uncle Joe's Guest House, now closed.

Weinstube Bar & Restaurant, near Senegambia. Smart, German-style 🍴 in same ownership as the Braustüble, Banjul.

Wine Pichet, Kololi Beach area, see Taj Mahal.

Yellow Gate, in backstreet south of New Town Rd, Bakau Nding (Bakau New Town). ☎92728. Chinese and Malay dishes.

Landing the fish at Bakau beach.

Yvonne Class Restaurant, Cape Point. The smartest and most expensive ✕ in The Gambia, and for a long way around. Opened 1990 under the supervision of owners Yvonne and Bill Marsh, in a building of distinctive design and décor. Most of the food is flown in from France weekly. Prices include an aperitif each, a bottle of wine, two cognacs and your taxi fare. ☎96222.

Ziegelhof, Kololi village, by the Keneba Hotel; German-owned ✕ with boutique.

NIGHTLIFE

The Gambia is no match for Benidorm when it comes to night life. The original casino has been closed for years with little prospect of reopening, but the Kololi Casino opened in 1992 near the Kairaba Hotel, offering gambling nightly from 2100. The Fajara and Amie's Beach hotels have casinos, but all other entertainment is tribal dancing and discos, confined to some of the hotels.

9: THE INDEPENDENT TRAVELLER

The Gambians' Gambia

THE GAMBIA HAS a number of hotels which don't appear in any tour operator's brochure. They range from the very good — to say excellent would be slightly over-generous — to the ghastly, with some surprises on the way.

This chapter contains all the accommodation not listed in the previous chapter, arranged alphabetically in the coastal area and then geographically from Yundum to Basse. Prices quoted are per person per night, without breakfast, unless stated otherwise.

BANJUL, BAKAU, SEREKUNDA:

ADONIS

Location: At the corner of Wellington and Hill streets, Banjul; ☎27262 (reception), 27264 (manager); **Tariff:** D150 single , D190 double

The Adonis gives its address as 23 Wellington St but the door is on its Hill St frontage. Built in 1960 by the Milky family, it is clean and smart, catering for west African businessmen. There are 21 rooms, each with air-conditioning and en-suite showers; a restaurant, but no bar.

APOLLO

Location: 33 Buckle St, **Address:** PO Box 419, Banjul; ☎28184; **Tariff:** sgl D120, dbl D250.

Closer to the Barra ferry than the Adonis, but slightly further from the city centre, the Apollo has a much smarter appearance, with an obvious security guard and a short flower-bordered path. Now shower and WC, the Apollo offered the first suites available on the local market.

The hotel opened in 1975 and has financed the Apollo 2 in Basse Santa Su; the interior is smart, but not up to the standard of the tourist hotels, and the unreliability of the city's electricity supply rules out any possibility of a lift.

There's a good restaurant room with a television set, but no bar.

ATLANTIC GUEST HOUSE

Location: 78 Atlantic Ave, Bakau, next to Tropic Gardens Hotel; ☎96237, **Tariff:** from D150 single.

Building conversion started in 1987 and was almost complete by 1993 with the addition of the garden restaurant. Lebanese owned, the guest house was briefly listed by The Gambia Experience as a first and last night stop for independent travellers.

BAKADAJI BUNGALOWS

Location: Kotu Point, near Palma Rima, ☎92307; **Tariff:** D250 double, b&b.

Beginning as a bar and restaurant, it graduated to a hotel in 1989 and had 12 rooms by 1992. Impressively smart, and Gambian owned.

BUNKOYO   *NO 4 IN FRONT OF TELEPONE NUMEAS 1/9/93*

Location: near Palma Rima hotel, **Address:** P.M.B. 274 Serekunda, ☎ & fax 93199; radio call signs G3DQL and C53GS; **Tariff:** from £15 single, b&b.   *463199*

The name is Mandinka for 'white house,' which this is, but it has no other identification. Owners Annie and Ernie Sumption opened in November 1989 with six double rooms, all with en-suite shower, leading into a large sitting room shared by guests and owners. Ernie gets several bookings from amateur radio enthusiasts. Extended in 1993 to 10 rooms.

CARLTON HOTEL

Location: Independence Ave, Banjul, facing the National Assembly; **Address:** PO Box 639, Banjul; ☎27258; **Tariff;** from D280, b&b.

The Carlton is a high-quality hotel for African businessmen which is also popular with Europeans. It's not in any tourist brochures, but several airlines have used it as a stopover for aircrews, although the trend is now towards lodging them at the Senegambia if they don't use discretionary time' and so fly out and back in the day.

CLIVE and MARCIA'S PLACE

Location: Katchikali, Bakau; ☎96654; bookings in the UK, ☎0737.772953 evenings.

Clive and Marcia Vare from Redhill have built four self-catering apartments each sleeping two or three people, in a small compound near the Katchikali sacred crocodile pit; fridge, cooker, kitchen and shower available in each apartment. Opened in 1991, early guests included two of the cast from *Emmerdale Farm*.

FOLLONKO

Location: Kartung, in The Gambia's southern coastal tip. Two double rooms, bar, restaurant, shower, flush toilet. Ideal for total isolation. Sgl D50, plus food.

Unashamed luxury awaits you at the Mansa Konko Guest House.

GAMBISSARA MOTEL

Location: near southern end of Kairaba Ave, Serekunda; ☎93114; **Tariff:** D125.

Opened in 1988 with 12 double rooms, all with en-suite shower and toilet. The motel has a bar and restaurant.

GOVERNMENT REST HOUSE, BARRA

Location: see map of Barra. No address nor telephone. **Tariff:** D10 per room per night; 3 rooms.

This is undoubtedly the cheapest lodging you can find within striking distance of Banjul and the coast; it's among the cheapest in the country. The rear-cover blurb on this book claims you can live on £1 a day: to do it you must sleep here and buy your food in the market at Barra, but if you are shopping for a Robinson Crusoe holiday with no nightlife you might enjoy yourself. The beach is a few minutes' walk away: you don't mind black sand and shingle?

The rest-house is a relic of colonial days and looks it; it's a timber bungalow on stilts with absolutely no services.

GREEN LINE MOTEL

Location: on the main road east of Serekunda centre; ☎94245; **Tariff:** D250 double.

A 'squeaky-clean' motel opened in January 1993 with 17 rooms, 10 of them with en-suite shower and toilet. The front is difficult to see, but there's ample parking space around the back. Owned by French-speaking Khalifé Wagih it is simply a motel – there's no restaurant or bar.

JULAKUNDA

Location: Mosque Rd, Serekunda, near a giant baobab, ☎91188; **Tariff:** D150 double.

A comfortable nine-room hotel on the first and second floors of a modern concrete-skeleton building overlooking the market. Can be noisy.

KANTORA

Location: Independence Drive, Banjul, almost opposite the National Assembly.

Closed for restoration in 1990 and not yet re-opened.

KENEBA HOTEL

Location: on unmade road from Senegambia to Kololi village; **Address:** PO Box 2957 Serekunda; ☎70093, fax 70095; **Tariff:** D175 double, b&b.

An African-style hotel with seven rondavels, each with en-suite toilet and set in colourful gardens. Gambian owner Banjugu Jawara opened for business in October 1992 and has a craft shop and restaurant on the premises.

KOLOLI TAVERN

Location: Kololi village, on tarmac road south-east of the old casino; ☎93410; **Address:** P.M.B. 273 Serekunda; **Tariff:** D150 single, b&b.

The tavern was built by its Gambian owners, a teacher, a farmer and a businessman, and opened in 1988. Accommodation for 28 people is in 14 rondavels or main rooms 10 minutes' walk from the beach. Gravity-fed bush showers available any time. Plenty of character, and a restaurant on the premises. Bush taxis to Serekunda or Senegambia pass the door, fare D2.

MONTROSE HOLIDAYS

Location: on edge of Bijilo village; **Address:** PO Box 2436, Serekunda; UK bookings through Gee Cross Travel Service, 219 Market St, Hyde, Ches, SK14 5RF, ☎061.368.7005. **Tariff:** £8.60 sgl, £14.50 dbl, b&b.

When Rosemary Long, woman's page editor of the Glasgow *Herald* met Gambian Rilwan Faal, romance blossomed. The Faals have several rondavels in their grounds by Bijilo Forest, 5 minutes from the beach and 20 minutes from Senegambia. Suzuki available for excursions.

The Kololi Tavern has shady gardens.

PARADISE INN

Location: beside Kololi Tavern; **Address:** PO Box 493 Serekunda; ☎90895; **Tariff:**D210 double.

Blackpool market trader Frank and former Jersey hotelier Sheila opened the self-built Paradise Inn in November 1992, with 5 rooms, each with en-suite washbasin; toilet and showers are separate. Smart – and with a bar. Bush taxis pass the door.

SERAKUNDA MOTEL

Location: Turn off main road by Serrakunda Modern Bakery onto Musa Dukureh Rd; motel is 100m on left; **Address:** PO Box 384, Serekunda, ☎92780; **Tariff:** sgl 175, dbl D225.

Note the spelling of the name, which is different from the next entry in this list. The motel is clean, quiet, comfortable, with a bar and restaurant – and colour television.

SEREKUNDA HOTEL

Location: On main road in Serekunda's southern suburbs; **Tariff:** D150.

Readers report this hotel to be pleasantly smart.

TERANGA

Location: Hill St. Banjul, near the junction with Buckle St; **Tariff:** 11 rooms at D80, 14 at D90.

The hotel is difficult to recognise from the road and looks like an apartment block on the Spanish coast. Rooms are on three floors, and the flat roof gives a good view of the city. Redecorated and with toilets modernised, it's now at acceptable standard.

HOTEL VICTORIA, BARRA

Location: see map of Barra; **Tariff:** D60 double, D35 single.

This is an airy place in a once-smart concrete-skeleton building near the Texaco petrol pumps in Barra, but the only indication that it is a hotel is the word 'reception' over the door. There's a toilet with a bidet — but there's no mains water. No electricity either, and not all the 18 rooms have beds.

Y.M.C.A. HOSTEL

The reasonably-smart two-storey hostel is on the edge of the Kanifing industrial estate; ☎91419, 92647; address, PO Box 421 Banjul. **Tariff:** sgl D80, dbl D125, including breakfast; lunch and dinner optional, D30. Reductions for groups.

The hostel has 16 rooms, a 50-seat restaurant for guests and for special functions such as weddings and parties, and courts for basketball and volleyball. Profits are used to finance The Gambia YMCA in its charitable activities.

UP-COUNTRY HOTELS, from Yundum to Basse

TRAVELLERS' LODGE, SOMA

Location: On east side of main street, the Transgambia Highway, see map; **Tariff:** D50 per room.

Utterly basic. I slept here in 1988 and both beds collapsed under me; little improvements since. Why not try the next two entries for preference?

TRAVELLERS' LODGE, PAKALI N'DING

Location: In Pakali N'Ding, just north of Soma; **Tariff:** D80

Don't confuse this with the Soma Travellers' Lodge; it's in a different class. I've twice tried to get in during the day, but the lodge gate was locked. A reader reports the five two-bed huts to be basic but adequate; at least, they have character.

MANSA KONKO COMMISSIONER'S GUEST HOUSE and REGIONAL HEALTH TEAM GUEST HOUSE

Location: on opposite sides of the road just beyond the end of the tarmac road into Mansa Konko from the Transgambia Highway. **Tariff:** D100 per person.

Both buildings are relics of colonial times and intended for Government use – the president stays in them – but they're available to travellers on a first-come basis. The former has two double rooms with air-conditioning, lounge, bath, separate WC, kitchen with gas and electric stoves, fridge. Electricity available 0800-0200 punctually.

Considering where they are, these guest houses are absolute luxury.

EDDIE'S HOTEL, FARAFENNI

Location: On the north side of the unmade road leading west to Kerewan from the centre of Farafenni, 150 yards from the Transgambia Highway and beside the bush taxi depot; **Tariff:** see text.

Eddie's combined night club, restaurant and hotel, with its own generators, is the central point for the social life of Farafenni. The gate opens onto a large concrete yard where several local businessmen garage their trucks; ahead is the night club, open on Saturday evenings; on the left is the hotel and restaurant.

Most of the 25 rooms open onto the central garden of tropical plants; the most expensive eight rooms cost D160 single, D240 same-sex double. Some have air-conditioning.

The restaurant serves perfectly good meals, ranging from continental breakfast for D20 to a steak and chips dinner for D45.

Eddie was born in 1970 in The Gambia and educated in London; the hotel is owned by Eddie's grandfather, Lebanese-born Mr Tabar, who assured me the Senegalese ladies are not on the staff but are nonetheless there for male pleasures.

FANKANTA

Location: On Transgambia Highway, Farafenni, towards the ferry. I never saw this place and can merely report that I'm told it's absolutely basic.

DIVISIONAL COMMISSIONER'S GUEST HOUSE, GEORGETOWN

Location: At the north of Georgetown, opposite the police station; see map; **Tariff:** D100 per person.

This is an ideal rest house and if The Gambia had two or three more up-country it would be a great inducement for excursion organisers to exploit the Macarthy Island and Upper Rivier divisions of the country, at present neglected because of the poor infrastructure.

The rest house is a smart verandah-fronted bungalow in its own grounds, with mimosa and kapok trees nearby, but it shares a gateway with a larger and even more impressive building behind it: the notice at the gate reads "Divisional Commissioner's Office and Residence." The setting is idyllic, and the morning chorus of bulbuls turns it into a tropical paradise.

In the same design and specification as the other commissioner's guest houses, but this one has three double rooms, and electricity is available from 1400 to 0200. I found the place idyllic, but a reader has reported the fridge was ineffective, the water supply haphazard, the toilet unsavoury, and the air-conditioning burst into flames.

TRAVELLERS' LODGE, BANSANG

On the main road in the village centre, and easily missed. Locked during the day, so I cannot give details, but it looks like its namesake in Soma.

INTERNATIOAL TRYPANOTOLERANCE CENTRE, BANSANG

Location: Mile west of the hospital. Not normally open to tourists.

COMMISSIONER'S GUEST HOUSE, BANSANG

Location: 100m east of the hospital, turn left. Specification as for Mansa Konko but D50 per person per night.

JEM HOTEL, BASSE

Location: in urban area on Fatoto side of town.

Joy Lawson of Ramsgate, who has arranged many gifts to Gambian schools, is building a smart European-style hotel in Basse, planning 10 rooms initially, each with en-suite shower and toilet. The Jem is scheduled to open early in 1994 with a restaurant offering inter-national cuisine; for information in the UK ☎0843.586985 evenings.

LINGUERE MOTEL, BASSE

Gambian Louis Mendy is building this motel and plans to offer excursions into Senegal's Nyokolo Kobo National Park; for information ☎92321.

PLAZA HOTEL, BASSE

Location: see map. **Tariff:** around D60 per double room.

This six-room first-floor hotel is in a concrete building in the midst of Basse's bustling market. It has frequently been closed, so information is lacking.

HOTEL TERANGA, BASSE

Location: by the Gamtel office, see map; **Tariff:** from D50 per double room.

This eight-room concrete-built hotel is marginally above basic standards.

APOLLO 2, BASSE

Location: On the right of the main tarmac street on entering the village; **Tariff:** from D50 per person.

Reasonably clean, comfortabe and airy, but otherwise basic. The building is fairly new with the ubiquitous corrugated-iron roof, but with refreshingly high ceilings. The 'Apolo 2' which is what the sign outside says, has eight double rooms leading off a central area which runs the length of the hotel; washbasins are at the far end of the hall, and there are two basic toilets and a shower room in the yard. Air conditioning is occasionally available.

UP-COUNTRY TRAVEL

By river. It is unfortunate that in 1993 there is only way to reach Basse by river; aboard the tug *Hans* from Jangjangbure.

By air. In the winter of 1991-92 a light aircraft operated a service between Yundum and Basse: if this could continue it would help open the hinterland to tourism.

By road. You have the choice of Gambia Public Transport Corporation buses, which have improved considerably in the early 1990s; buses operated by Amdalaye Transport, the rival firm run by

Mr Mohammed Kebbeh, a leading businessman; or by bush taxi. Since 1991 and for the forseeable future the bus schedules have been disrupted by the collapse of the road surface between Brikama and Soma.

BUSH TAXIS

Most bush taxis are Peugeot 405 pick-up trucks with minibus bodies on the rear, and they're identical to the *matatus* of Kenya, Uganda and Tanzania. Three passengers squeeze in on the bench seat beside the driver, and up to 14 people force themselves into the minibus body through the door at the back; the conductor is usually a boy, for nimbleness and economy of space and weight, but he needs to be strong enough to haul himself onto the bush taxi's roof to load and offload the cargo, which can weight up to 5cwt (250kg) and include live goats.

Timetable. Bush taxis don't operate to a timetable; they go either when they're full or when the driver is tired of waiting for anybody else to come along. If you're the first passenger you may wait three hours; if you're the last, you'll be hustled aboard and on the road within seconds.

Bush taxis cover the entire country wherever there is demand, but in Serekunda and Banjul they are usually replaced by the larger minibuses, whose condition ranges from ancient to pristine. The route between Bakau and Serekunda is now operated by conventional taxis – private cars – but make certain you're paying the D2 per-person fare of the African taxi and not the D40 for exclusive use of the tourist

The Divisional Commissioner's Guest House in Georgetown is my idea of paradise, but other readers differ.

The Apollo 2 Hotel in Basse is on the far right. Hundreds of egrets roost in the village's mango trees.

taxi. The Serekunda depot is the largest in the country and overflows onto surrounding streets.

Fares. Fares are cheap, but not as cheap as on the buses. Serekunda to Soma costs around D30, and on to Georgetown an extra D25; you may be charged extra for luggage. The annual road tax on these bush taxis is D150.

BUSES

GPTC. The GPTC's main depot is on a back road in the industrial estate at Kanifing, north-east of Serekunda, where the firm's administrative offices, workshops and main fuel supplies are located; I have noted other fuel depots at Soma and Barra.

GPTC had the monopoly of public transport in the capital, with resulting overcrowding; you will have a better chance of getting a seat if you make your way to the city's main bus depot in the Half Die (see the map of Banjul) rather than wait at any of the bus stops, particularly the one by MacCarthy Square, temporarily closed by the relaying of the city's streets.

Fares. Passengers enter the bus at the rear door, buy their tickets from the conductor seated inside a steel-wire cage, and rush for seats. Then the aisle is packed tight, then five more people squeeze aboard, and finally ten others find space that everyone else had missed. Fares are cheap by European standards: you can travel the length of the country by bus for D50.

Timetable. There is no national timetable for either GPTC or Amdalaye, and if there were the road conditions would play havoc with it. When I asked for the GPTC timetable in 1988 I was probably the first person to make such a request; in 1991 I had this list of departure times from the three main depots, which is still viable; there are no times of arrival.

From BANJUL (all calling at Soma):
0700, Sabi
0745, Gambissara
0800, Basse (express)
0830, Numuyel
0915, Basse
1010, Garowal
1100, Kulari
1200, Sutukung
1330, Karantaba
1415, Dankunku
1500, Sutukung
1630, Soma.

There are appropriate return services from all up-country villages but you will need to ask locally for the departure times; suggestably ask the bus driver on your outward journey.

From KANIFING Industrial estate:
These services are purely local and for people travelling to and from work. The service starts at 0615 to Banjul and ends 1700 to Bundung. However, several long-distance buses call at the depot for fuel and you may be able to get a seat.

From SOMA:
0700, Banjul
0845, Banjul
0900, Basse
1015, ⎫
1130, ⎪
1145, ⎪
1230, ⎬ Banjul and Basse
1315, ⎪
1415, ⎪
1515, ⎪
1700, ⎭
1815, Dankunku
1910, Sutukung.

Other services: Banjul to Tanji and Gunjor; frequent services to Bakau and Serekunda.

On the **north shore** there are services linking Barra and the Senegalese frontier; and linking Barra and Darsilami (Kerewan ferry) via northern, central and southern (Juffure) routes; another service links Kerewan and Lamin Koto (Georgetown) via Farafenni.

DISTANCES BY ROAD

Banjul–Soma	4½ hrs	181km
Banjul–MacCarthy Island	7½ hrs	306km
Banjul–Basse	9 hrs	373km
Banjul–Fatoto	10½ hrs	415km
Pakali Ba–MacCarthy Island		79km
Soma–MacCarthy Island		125km

Passengers streaming off the Barra ferry in Banjul. This was a telephoto shot taken from cover.

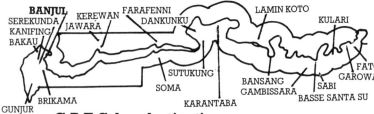

G.P.T.C. bus destinations.

Minibuses usually operate around Serekunda and Banjul, but this one was up-country.

AMDALAYE BUS SCHEDULE

Banjul – Basse:
Depart Banjul 0730, 0830; arrive Basse 1500, 1600.

Basse – Banjul:
Depart Basse 0730, 0830; arrive Banjul 1500, 1600.
Picks up on road and diverts to Mansa Konko, Janjangbure Island south ferry for Georgetown, Bansang.

Barra – Amdalaye (Senegal border):
Hourly service each way, 0700-2000.

Farafenni – Kerewan:
Three-hourly frequency each direction.

Banjul – Serekunda:
Frequent service each way at morning and evening peak times; depots at Half Die, Banjul, and main depot by Serekunda market.

DISTANCES BY RIVER

From Banjul in miles (kms) to:

Albreda, 15 (24); Kerewan, 37 (59); Tendaba Camp, 61 (99); Bambali (Elephant Island), 94 (152); Kaur, 113 (182); Kudang Tenda, 129 (208); Kuntaur, 141 (228); Georgetown 164 (265); Bansang, 174 (281); Karantaba Tenda (near Mungo Park Memorial), 186 (300); Diabugu Tenda, 206 (332); Basse Duma Su, 224 (361).

THE HIGHWAY SYSTEM

The streets of Banjul, Bakau and Serekunda are tarred, as are the roads linking the communities, and the route from Serekunda to Sukuta. The country's main road from Serekunda to Basse was laid in two stages, the first stretch to Soma built just after independence, using cockle shells that had been piling up for generations. This surface is now breaking up and will involve the rebuilding of the entire section.

The Gambia has 190 miles (306km) of tarred roads, including the Transgambia Highway north and south of the ferry, the road north from Barra to Amdalaye on the Senegalese border, south from Mandina Ba (east of Brikama) to the border, the spur road to Yundum Airport, and in Mansa Konko.

The Highway. The road from Banjul to Serekunda has been in a poor state for years, but is now a superb four-lane dual carriageway (divided highway) equal to the best in Europe. One carriageway was completed hours before the dawn of 4th October 1989, the 25th anniversary of independence, and the second carriageway was in use soon after.

Gambia Dam? Stretches of the Transgambia Highway, particularly north and south of the ferry, are in poor repair, but the landing stages were rebuilt in 1989, thus silencing any rumours about creating a barrage across the river a little way upstream.

Moving villages. The highway from Soma to Basse was begun in 1979 and the President officially declared it open in 1982. It is well-engineered, which involved the straightening of some of the bends in the original laterite track, which in turn has left some communities a little too far from the new road. In the coming years several of these villages will move closer to the tarmac, as two or three men can carry a corrugated-iron house easily, and the traditional compounds of elephant grass, bamboo and mud, must be rebuilt every few years in any event.

All other roads in the country are unsurfaced tracks, liable to turn to mud in the rains and frequently covered in dust in the tourist season.

In 1992 work began on regrading the laterite road on the north bank from Lamin Koto by Jangjangbure to Madina Taibatu north of Basse.

THE FERRIES

Banjul-Barra. The Banjul to Barra ferry service operates one drive-through vessel with a second as standby; each can carry several hundred foot passengers, including a few pickpockets and smugglers, and vehicles up to the largest lorry.

Sailings from Banjul are: 0800–1000–1200–1400–1600–1800.

Sailings from Barra are: 0900–1100–1300–1500–1700–1930.

The crossing takes 30 minutes.

Fares. Fares were revised on 1 October 1990 and are now: foot passenger D3; cyclist D5; motor cyclist D10; car and driver D50; taxi and driver D60; Land-Rover and driver D70; and lorry (truck) more than 30 tonnes D368; tariff trebled for foreign-registered vehicles.

If you're lucky enough to have your own transport, don't wait for the last crossing of the day as your ticket doesn't guarantee you a passage. Motorists must buy their ticket at a weighbridge 1.5 miles (2km) out along the road to Dakar, but foot passengers and cyclists pay as they come aboard.

The steel German-built vessels were introduced in 1979 to replace the three original wooden ferries and there was a national outcry when the officials realised the ferries would not fit into their berths at certain states of the tide. By the way, if you have no other means of seeing the dolphins at play, you could always take a passage on the Barra ferry.

Transgambia Highway. In the summer of 1988 the Japanese-built *Barajally* and the *James Island* came into service on the Transgambia ferry, replacing two ferries built in Brightlingsea, Essex. The new ferries are each 150 feet (46m) long overall and 30 feet (10m) in the beam, capable of carrying vehicles weighing 150 tons as well as 100 passengers. The last crossing is around 2000hrs, and the tariff is trebled for foreign-registered vehicles, an annoyance to Senegalese traffic.

Even the ferryboat at Kerewan on the north shore has a corrugated iron roof!

The crossing is busy as it not only links the Casamance region of Senegal with the remainder of the country, but it is also a vital link on the Lagos (Nigeria) to Nouakchott (Mauritania) stretch of the African highway system.

Long queues of lorries sometimes build up on one or both shores, so several enterprising businessmen have set up stalls to cater for their needs.

Foot passengers are spared these frustrations as other enterprising Gambians operate motor-driven pirogues — that's the dug-out canoe with extra sides, the kind of boat you also see on the beaches — and will ferry you across, 15 at a time, for a dalasi each. It's a very picturesque setting, but cameras are distinctly unwelcome. The bush taxi fare from the ferry to either Soma or Farafenni is D3; the ferry itself costs D2 for a pedestrian, D7 for car and driver.

Jarreng — Carrol's Wharf.

This little-known ferry operates from a wharf near Jarreng (midway between Pakali Ba and Kudang), along a backwater beside the paddy fields of Pappa Island, then across the main river to Carrol's Wharf from where a track leads north to Charmen. Motor-cycles are the largest vehicles carried, for a fare of D3, the same as pedestrians.

Kuntaur. A vehicle ferry crosses from Kuntaur on the north shore; pedestrians D1, cars D20.

Passengers on the cable-operated ferry haul themselves across to MacCarthy Island.

The new wharf at Bansang is for loading groundnuts. A private-enterprise ferry is in competition with the main service.

MacCarthy Island (Georgetown), south. The main channel of the Gambia River goes to the north of MacCarthy, so there is no problem in having a steel cable stretched loosely across the southern channel. This cable runs through pulleys set at waist level along one side of a pontoon, and the passengers provide their own motive power. The pontoon is capable of carrying buses and bush taxis, but doesn't; a local taxi will carry you across Jangjangbure Island for D1, but the mile-long walk along the tarmac road is pleasant. The fare for pedestrians is D1, for cars D20, Land-Rovers D25, return – if you come back the same day.

MacCarthy Island (Georgetown), north. The ferry is an ancient diesel-powered timber vessel with a hump-backed deck and a big ramp at her square bows, and she's capable of carrying four cars or two mini-buses. Following 1988 reorganisation on the ferry system, the schedule is now:

> **From Georgetown:**
> 0800 — 0930 — 1130 — 1415 — 1530 — 1730
> **From Lamin Koto:**
> 0815 — 1030 — 1230 — 1430 — 1630 — 1745.

Pedestrians pay D1, cars D20, Land-Rovers D25.

Bansang. The Bansang ferry, provided by Action Aid, is identical to the Georgetown south pontoon, with the same fares.

Basse. A new all-steel ferry operates on the Basse crossing, with the same schedule as above, beginning at Basse, and the same fares.

Pirogue ferries. Backpackers can use unscheduled pirogues on Kerewan, Transgambia, Bansang and Basse crossings, and also — I hear — travel by pirogue between Bansang and the upstream village of Karantaba Tenda.

Fatoto. This last ferry across the Gambia River carries pedestrians, cyclists, and cattle — though many of the latter swim alongside the vessel. The three craft available are welded from flat sections of sheet steel and the ferryman Sule Keta and his family propel themselves across the river by paddle or pole. The fare is D1.

Kerewan. The Kerewan ferry across the Jowara Bolong on the North Bank is an older wooden-decked craft, working on the same fare and schedule already given, starting from Kerewan.

THE GAMBIA BY CYCLE

Cycling around The Gambia? Ridiculous! A couple I met near Farafenni assured me it was not such a ridiculous idea. The country is small so, unless you have designs on penetrating deep into Senegal, you could cover almost every mile of tarmac in a fortnight's leisurely cycling.

The main hazard is the poor road between Brikama and Soma where, for several miles, all traffic drives on the verge; cyclists may be safer in the middle of the road, going around the holes and keeping an ear on vehicles approaching from behind – or going to Soma by bush taxi.

There are few hills, traffic is light, and you have an ideal opportunity to see the wildlife, including some of the shyer animals.

Preparations. Ideally you should be with one companion; make the party too big and you might hit accommodation problems. You'll need a sturdy cycle and you'll obviously have to carry all the spare parts you could possibly want, including extra tyres.

Climate. The main hazard will be the climate. The couple I met had planned to be on the road at 0800 and break for the heat of the day by 1100, with another two hours from 1600. The schedule had to be flexible but they were careful not to tire themselves or to risk dehydration.

They carried dried foods, a small stove and saucepans, lightweight sleeping bags, water carriers, a change of clothing, and plenty of candles. They never travelled by night — the dark continent really *is* the dark continent when there's no moon — and they had no difficulties in finding somewhere to sleep in any of the small up-country villages: a few words with the head man, or sign language on occasion, always brought them the offer of a spare room or a spare hut in a compound.

The Fatoto ferryman with some of his children.

Wellington St, Banjul, is showing signs of affluence.

Banjul's Anglican Cathedral is much smaller than its Catholic counterpart.

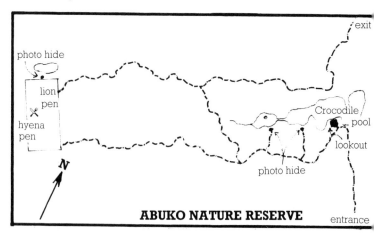

10: WILDLIFE IN THE GAMBIA

Birds and other creatures

THE COUNTRYSIDE IS NOT AFLUTTER WITH BIRDS, but you cannot fail to see vultures circling over the markets and settling in the upper branches of the baobabs; you will see the familiar European swallows circling over the treetops, and the bright blue flash of an Abyssinian roller swooping through the bush.

The keen birdwatcher will want to go deeper into the bush and to creep along the bolongs in a paddle-driven pirogue to see pelicans, herons, and other birds of the river and swamp. This is where he will appreciate a specialist organised expedition such as those offered by Gamtours, Sunshine Holidays and Black & White Safaris. And, from late 1993, by Gambia Options with its two-week safaris to the far end of the country, and beyond, the only company to use the services of Mass Cham, the country's leading native-born ornithologist. Even if the visitor isn't planning a night away from the comfort of a tourist hotel, he or she should certainly visit the Abuko Nature Reserve, independently or in a party.

Eddie Brewer, who campaigned to establish the reserve and was the first Director of Wildlife Conservation in The Gambia, urged the country to market itself to the world's tourist industry as Africa's leading nation for birdwatchers, but cautioned that development on the coast be planned with conservation in mind, not least by leaving stands of virgin bush between hotels.

Apart from in Abuko, wildlife is all around you in a wide variety of habitats: the beach, the mangrove swamps, the rice paddies, the bush, the salt pans, the urban areas, and the hotel gardens – particularly the Senegambia Hotel. Considering birdlife alone, frequency of sighting depends upon many factors, including accessibility of habitat, season (many birds have brighter plumage during the rainy season, when they breed), the bird's shyness, it markings, the time of day, and the specie population.

In this checklist, zoological names and French and German translations have been taken from *A Field Guide to the Birds of West Africa*, and the ✝ symbol indicates the commonest winter birds.

Babbler, brown *Turdoides plebejus* cratérope brun Schuppendrossling.
Barbet, bearded *Lybius dubius* barbican à poitrine rouge

These hyenas keep away from man even at feeding time in Abuko.

Senegalfurchenschnabel.
Barbet, Vieillot's *Lybius vieilloti* barbut de Vieillot — Blutbrust Bartvogel.
Bateleur *Terathropicus ecaudatus* bateleur — Gaukler.
Bee-eater, European *Merops apiaster* guêpier d'Europe — Bienenfresser.
Bee-eater, little *Merops pusillus* guêpier nain — Zwergspint.
Bee-eater, swallow-tailed *Merops hirundineus* guêpier à queue d'hirondelle — Schwalbenschwanzspint.
Bulbul, common *Pycnonotus barbatus* bulbul commun — Graubulbul.
Bulbul, white-vented.
Bunting, cinnamon-breasted rock *emberiza tahapisi* bruant canelle — Bergammer.
Buzzard, lizard *Kaupifalco monogrammicus* buse unibande — Sperberbussard.
Camaroptera, grey-backed *Camaroptera brachyura* camaroptère à tête grise — Meckergrasmücke.
Cordon-bleu, red-cheeked *Estrilda bengala* cordon-bleu — Schmetterlingsastrid.
Cormorant, long-tailed.
Coucal, Senegal *Centropus senegalensis* coucal du Sénégal — Spornkuckuc.
Crombec *Sylvietta* crombec — Sylvietta.

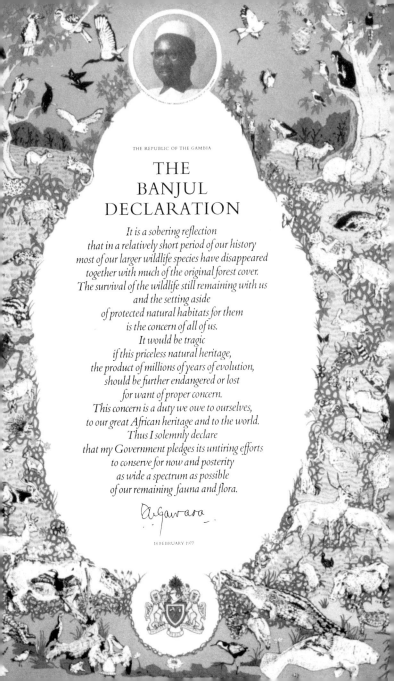

THE REPUBLIC OF THE GAMBIA

THE
BANJUL
DECLARATION

*It is a sobering reflection
that in a relatively short period of our history
most of our larger wildlife species have disappeared
together with much of the original forest cover.
The survival of the wildlife still remaining with us
and the setting aside
of protected natural habitats for them
is the concern of all of us.
It would be tragic
if this priceless natural heritage,
the product of millions of years of evolution,
should be further endangered or lost
for want of proper concern.
This concern is a duty we owe to ourselves,
to our great African heritage and to the world.
Thus I solemnly declare
that my Government pledges its untiring efforts
to conserve for now and posterity
as wide a spectrum as possible
of our remaining fauna and flora.*

DJ Jawara

18 FEBRUARY 1977

Cuckoo, common *Cuculus canoris vulgaris* coucou gris — Kuckuck.

Cuckoo-shrike, white-breasted *Coracina pectoralis* echenilleur à ventre blanc — Weissbrustraupenfänger.

Curlew *Numenius arquata* courlis cendré — Grosser Brachvogel.

Cut-throat.

Darter, African *Anhinga rufa* anhinga d'Afrique — Afrikanischer Schlagenhalsvogel.

✦ **Dove, laughing** *Streptopelia senegalensis* tourterelle maillée — Palmtaube.

Dove, Namanga.

Dove, vinaceous *Streptopelia vinacea* tourterelle vineuse — Röteltaube.

Drongo, glossy-backed *Dicrurus adsimilis* drongo brillant — Trauerdrongo.

Eagle, short-toed *Circaetus gallicus* circaète Jean-le-Blanc — Schlagenadler.

Eagle, west African river *Haliaetus vocifer* aigle pêcheur — Schreiseeadler.

Egret, great white *Egretta alba* grande aigrette — Silberreiher.

✦ **Egret, intermediate.**

✦ **Egret, little** *Egretta garzetta* aigrette garzette — Seidenreiher.

Eremomela, green-backed *Eremomela pusilla* erémomèle à dos vert — Graukappeneremomela.

Finch, Senegal indigo *Vidua chalybeata* combassou du Sénégal — Rotfussatlaswitwe.

Fire-finch, lavender *Estrilda caerulescens* queue de vinaigre — Schönbürzel.

Fire-finch, red-billed.

✦ **Fire-finch, Senegal** *Lagonostica senegala* amarante commun — Senegalsamarant.

Flycatcher, black *Melaenornis edolioides* gobe-mouche drongo — Schieferschwartzerdrongoschnäpper.

Flycatcher, dusky blue *Muscicapa comitata* gobe-mouche ardoisé — Stuhlmanschnäpper.

Flycatcher, paradise *Terpsiphone viridis* moucherolle de paradis — Afrikanischer Paradiesenschnäpper.

Flycatcher, Senegal puff-back *Batis senegalensis* gobe-mouche soyeux du Sénégal — Senegalschnäpper.

Flycatcher, swamp *Muscicapa aquatica* gobe-mouche des marais — Sumpfschnäpper.

Francolin, double-spurred *Francolinus clappertoni* francolin commun — Doppelspornfrankolin.

Goose, spur-winged *Plectropterus gambensis* canard armé — Sporenganz.

The best place to see crocodiles is in the sacred pits; these specimens were at Bakau.

Goshawk, chanting *Melierax metabates* autour chanteur — Graubürzelsinghabicht.

Goshawk, gabar *Melierax gabar* autour gabar — Gabarhabicht.

Greenshank *Tringa nebularia* chevalier aboyeur — Grünschenkel.

Hammerkop *Scopus umbretta* ombrette — Hammerkopf.

Harrier, marsh *Circus aeruginosus* busard des roseaux — Rohrweihe.

Harrier, pallid *Circus macrourus* busard pâle — Steppenweihe.

Harrier-eagle, banded *Circaetus cinerascens* circaète cendré — Bandschlangenadler.

Harrier-eagle, brown *Circaetus cinereus* circaète brun — Einfarbschlangenadler.

Harrier-hawk *Polyboroides radiatus* petit serpentaire — Höhlenweihe.

Hawk-eagle, long-crested *Lophaetus occipitalis* aigle huppard — Schlopfadler.

Helmet-shrike, long-crested *Prionops plumata* bagadais casqué — Brillenwürger.

Helmet-shrike, straight-crested.

Heron, black-headed *Ardea melanocephala* héron melanocéphale — Schwarzhalsreiher.

Heron, goliath *Ardea goliath* héron goliath — Goliathreiher.

Heron, green-backed *Butorides striatus* héron à dos vert — Mangrovereiher.

Heron, grey *Cinerea* héron cendré — Fischreiher (Graureiher).
Heron, purple *Ardea purpurea* héron pourpré — Purpurreiher.
Heron, squacco *Ardeola ralloides* héron crabier — Rallenreiher.
Heron, western reef *Egretta gularis* aigrette dimorphe — Küstenreiher.
Honey-guide, black-throated *Indicator indicator* grand indicateur — Gross Honiganzeiger.
Hornbill, grey *Tockus nasutus* petit calao à bec noir — Grautoko.
Hornbill, Abyssinian ground *Bucorvus abyssinicus* grand calao d'Abyssinie — Sudanhornrabe.
✦ **Hornbill, red-beaked** *Tockus erythrorhynchus* petit calao à bec rouge — Rotschnabeltoko.
Ibis, sacred *Threskiornis aethiopica* ibis sacré — Heiliger Ibis.
Kestrel *Falco tinnunculus* crécerelle — Turmfalke.
Kestrel, grey *Falco ardiosiaceus* faucon ardoisé — Graufalke.
Kingfisher, blue-breasted *Halcyon malimbica* martin-chasseur à poitrine bleue — Zügelliest.
Kingfisher, grey-headed *Halcyon leucocephala* martin-chasseur à tête grise — Graukopfliest.
Kingfisher, malachite *Alcedo cristata* martin-pêcheur huppé — Malachiteisvogel.
Kingfisher, pied *Ceryle rudis* martin-pêcheur pie — Graufischer.
Kingfisher, striped *Halcyon chelicuti* martin-chasseur strié — Streifenliest.
✦ **Kite, black** *Milvus migrans* milan noir — Schwarzmilan.
Lapwing, wattled.
Long-claw, yellow-throated *Macronyx croceus* alouette sentinelle — Gelpkehlpieper.
Mannikin, bronze *Lonchura cucullata* spermète nonette — Kleinelsterchen.
Oriole, African golden *Priolatus auratus* loriot doré — Schwarzohrpirol.
Osprey *Pandion haliaetus* balbuzard pêcheur — Fischadler.
Owl, scops *Otus scops* petit-duc africain — Zwergohreule.
Owlet, pearl-spotted *Glaucidium perlatum* chevêchette perlèe — Perlkauz.
Parakeet, ringed.
Parakeet, Senegal long-tailed *Psittacula krameri* perruche à collier — Halsbandsittich.
Parrot, brown-necked *Poicephalus robustus* perroquet robuste — Kappapagei.
Parrot, Senegal *Poicephalus senegalus* youyou — Morhenkopf.
Pelican, pink-backed *Pelecanus rufescens* pélican gris — Rötelpelikan.
✦ **Pigeon, Bruce's green.**

There is a crocodile in this picture at Abuko's Crocodile Pool, but you would need binoculars to see it. The scenery is splendid.

Pipit, plain-backed *Anthus leuciphrys* pipit à a dos roux — Braunrückenpeiper.

Plantain-eater, grey *Crinifer piscator* touraco gris — Schwarzschwanzlärmvogel.

Plover, black-headed *Vanellus tectus* vanneau à tête noire — Schwarzkopfkiebitz.

Plover, grey *Pluvialis squatarola* pluvier argenté — Kiebitzregenpfeifer.

Plover, Senegal wattled *Vanellus senegallus* vanneau caronculé — Senegalkiebitz.

Pratincole *Glareola pratincola* glaréole á collier — Brachschwalbe.

Prinia, west African *Prinia subflava* fauvètte-riotelet commune — Rahmbrustprinie.

Redshank *Tringa totanus* chevalier gambtete — Rotschenkel.

Redstart *Phoenicurus phoenicurus* rouge-queue à front blanc — Gartenrotschwanz.

Robin-chat, white-crowned *Cossypha albicapilla* grand cossyphe á tête blanche — Schuppenkopfrötel.

🐦 **Roller, Abyssinian** *Coracias abyssinica* rollier d'Abyssinie — Senegalracke.

Roller, broad-billed *Eurystomus glaucurus* rollier africain — Zimtroller.

Ruff *Philomachus pugnax* chevalier combattante — Kampfläufer.

Sandgrouse, four-banded *Pterocles quadricinctus* ganga de la Gambie — Buschflughuhn.

Sandpiper, common *Tringa hypoleucos* chevalier guignette — Flussuferläufer.

Sandpiper, wood *Tringa glareola* chevalier sylvain — Bruchwasserläufer.

Shikra *Accipter badius* epervier shikra — Schikra.

Shrike, Barbary *Laniarius barbarus* gonolek de Barbarie — Scharlachwürger.

Shrike, black-headed bush.

Shrike, brubu *Nilaus afer* pie-grèche bru-bru — Brubru.

Shrike, Gambian puff-back *Dryoscopus gambensis* pie-grièche subla de la Gambie — Waldschneeballwürger.

Shrike, woodchat *Lanius senator* pie-grièche à tête rousse — Rotkopfwürger.

Silverbill, warbling *Lonchura malabarica* bec d'argent — Silberschnabelchen.

Snipe, common *Gallinago gallinago* bécasse des marais — Bekassine.

Sparrow, grey-headed *Passer griseus* moineau gris — Graukopfsperling.

🐦 **Starling, long-tailed glossy** *Lamprotornis caudatus* merle

métallique à long queue — Langschwanzglanzstar.
Starling, purple-headed glossy *Lamprotornis purpureus* merle métallique à tête pourprée — Samtglanzstar.
Stone-partridge *Ptilopachus petrosus* poule de rocher — Felsenrebhuhn.
Stork, white-necked.
Stork, wooly-necked *Ciconia episcopus* cigogne episcopale — Wohlhalsstorch.
Sunbird, beautiful long-tailed *Nectarinia pulchella* soui-manga à long queue — Elfennektarvogel.
Sunbird, pygmy long-tailed *Anthreptes platura* petit soui-manga à long queue — Erznektarvogel.
Sunbird, scarlet-breasted *Nectarinia senegalensis* soui-manga à poitrine rouge — Rotbrustglanzköpfchen.
Swallow, European *Hirundo rustica* hirondelle de cheminée — Rauchschwalbe.
Swallow, mosque *Hirundo senegalensis* hirondelle à ventre rouge — Senegalschwalbe.
Swallow, red-rumped *Hirundo daurica* hirondelle rousseline — Rötelschwalbe.
Swift, little African *Apus affinis* martinet à dos blanc — Haussegler.
Tchagra, black-crowned *Tchagra senegala* tchagra — Tchagra.
Tern, gull-billed *Sterna nilotica* sterne hansel — Lachsseeschwalbe.

The ndama cow is immune to the tsetse fly. Kola palms are in the background.

Tern, royal *Sterna maxima* sterne royale — Königseeschwalbe.
Tern, white-ringed black *Sterna leucoptera* guiffet leucoptère — Weissflügelseeschwalbe.
Thick-knee, Senegal *Burhinius senegalensis* oedicnème du Sénégal — Senegaltriel.
Vulture, hooded *Neophron monachus* percnoptère brun — Kappengeier.
Vulture, palm-nut *Gypohierax angloensis* vauture palmiste — Palmgeier.
Vulture, white-backed *Gyps bengalensis* gyps africain — Weissrückengeier.
Wagtail, white *Motacilla alba* gergeronnette grise— Bachstelze.
Warbler, desert fan-tail *Cisticola aridula* cisticole du désert — Kalaharizistensänger.
Warbler, sup-alpine *Sylvia cantillans* fauvette passerinette — Weissbartgrasmücke.
Wheatear *Oenanthe oenanthe* traquet motteux — Steinschmätzer.
Whimbrel *Numenius phaeopus* courlis courlieu — Regenbrachvogel.
Whinchat *Saxicola rubetra* traquet tarier –– Braunkehlchen.
White-eye, yellow-throated *Zosterops senegalensis* oiseau-lunettes jaune — Senegal Brillenvogel.
Whydah, pin-tailed *Vidua macroura* veuve Dominicaine — Dominikanewitwe.
Wood-hoopoe, green.
Wood-hoopoe, lesser *Phoeniculus aterrimus* petit moqueur noir — Zwergbaumhopf.
Woodpecker, cardinal *Dendropicos fuscescens* pic cardinal — Kardinalspecht.
Woodpecker, fine-spotted *Campethera punctuligera* pic à taches noires — Punktchenspecht.
Woodpecker, grey *Mesopicos goertae* pic gris — Graubrustspecht.
Woodpecker, least grey *Dendropicos gambonensis* petit pic gris — Wüstenspecht.

Birds of the shoreline... The mangrove swamps and bolongs behind Banjul are home for a surprising number of genuses, many of which are familiar to European birdwatchers. A walk along the Bund Road in Banjul brings you within binocular distance of herons, egrets, pelicans, 12 sub-species of plover, sandpipers, several of the terns, and in April 1988 a solitary avocet. The flamingos have now gone.

At Toll Point near the Wadner Beach Hotel, there are several gull and plover species mixing with stints and stilts, plus shikra and shrike which have wandered from the bush.

The Cape Coast mudflats have the gulls and waders one would

expect, but there are also Barbary shrike, osprey, two vulture sub-species and several other raptors.

...and of the river. The mangrove swamps stretching inland to beyond the Transgambia Highway ferry have most of the world's species of waders, as well as storks and ibises, herons and egrets, rails, crakes, dabchicks and divers, mingling with some of the exotic bush species such as the cordon bleu and several sunbirds, the Old World's answer to the humming bird.

The drier south bank in its middle reaches is a splendid habitat for exotic species such as the secretary bird, the nightjar, the whydah,and several cuckoos; the semi-arid zone beginning around the Kai Hai Islands is home for the Sudan bustard and the francolin as well as several bush species and waders, confirming The Gambia as a meeting-place of genuses from widely differing habitats ranging from the sub-polar to the tropic, from the mountains to the moors, and from the deserts to the mudflats.

Banjul Declaration. The Gambia is no longer the place to come to see the big game which, poachers permitting, you can still find in east Africa. President Jawara pledged himself in his Independence Day speech in 1977 to conserve as much as possible of the country's 'remaining fauna and flora,' a promise which has come to be known as the Banjul Declaration. Action followed, with the passing of the Wildlife Conservation Act later that year which banned hunting and any trading in wild animal products — yet Senegal has six legalised hunting areas, one just over the border from Farafenni and Kaur, and another at Toubacouta on the road from Barra to Dakar.

Vultures are common. These are in the bus depot at Soma.

ABUKO NATURE RESERVE

The British conservationist Eddie Brewer proposed in 1967 the establishment of the Abuko Nature Reserve, which President Jawara created within six weeks. Eddie became director of the Wildlife Conservation Department shortly before the president made his Banjul Declaration on 18 February 1977, and soon Eddie's daughter Stella embarked on her great mission to rehabilitate some of the unfortunate chimpanzees of this world, which she wrote about in her book *Forest Dwellers,* and described on several television programmes. The Brewers have now gone, Eddie into retirement, and Stella has taken her chimps to the Baboon Islands by Kuntaur, territory closed to other human visitors.

Entry. The entry fee is D15 for an adult, D5 for a child, from 1 Oct to 31 May; D10 and D2 at other times. The gate opens at 0800 daily and closes at 1800. ♿ Visitors in wheelchairs, the elderly and the very young, may ask at the pay desk for permission to drive to the cluster of buildings at the top of the reserve, but everybody else walks the 1.8 miles (2.9km) of path through the virgin forest — and that is the essence of your visit to Abuko.

Waterworks. In 1916 a small pumping station was built by the natural pools which now form the reserve's focal point, supplying drinking water to the tiny villages of Bakau and Fajara; the Bakau and Serekunda area map shows the pipeline, a part of which now runs under Kairaba Avenue, which was known as Pipeline Road until 1989. The area remained undisturbed, and was saved for posterity by the reserve.

You should calculate on two hours minimum for Abuko, but anybody with an interest in nature would find two days not enough. The winding footpath leads through jungle, the only true jungle you will see in The Gambia, where oil palms rise to 90ft (30m) and where lianas and strangler figs form a three-dimensional undergrowth amid gnarled and contorted trees.

Birds sing from the branches all around, the occasional rustle of leaf litter announces a troup of monkeys, and everywhere you will see webs spanning gaps up to 15ft (5m) wide, spun by spiders with legspans up to 4in (10cm). Monitor lizards a metre long sunbathe on the path, and snakes slide away at the slightest sound.

Crocodiles. The crocodile pool is the most dramatic sight, where a croc and an African python have been seen in mortal combat; in the dry season you may see up to 30 crocodiles at once.

At the south-western end of the reserve's original 180 acres (73ha) is an enclosure with refreshment room, toilets, the animal orphanage, and pens for spotted hyena and lion. I've been in the hyena enclosure during feeding time, but I wouldn't disturb the lions during *their* meals. British Caledonian Airways gave the older male, Mac, in 1982, and brought his mate Dylise from Britain in 1984; she came from the Longleat Safari Park near Bath, England. Beyond the enclosure lie the 72 acres (29ha) of the 1978 extension, mostly open grassland like the surrounding countryside.

November and December are the best months to see the wide range of butterflies, and the end of the rainy season brings out the most wild flowers.

The reserve's booklet lists some of Abuko's smaller residents, and a few of the 280 species of birds seen here, but I omit those which are also in the Tendaba check-list:

Animals:

Antelope, harnessed (bushbok), *Tragelaphus scriptus,* guid harnaché – Schirrantilope.

Duiker, Grimm's, *Sylvicapra grimmia,* céphalope de Grimm – Kronenducker.

Ground squirrel, striped, *Xerus erythropus,* rat palmiste – Gestreiftes Erdhörnchen.

Monkey, green vervet, *Cercopithecus aethiops,* singe grivet – Grüne Meerkatze.

Monkey, red patas, *Erythrocebus patas,* singe rouge – Husarenaffe.

Monkey, western red colobus, *Colobus (Piliocolobus) badius,* colobe bai d'Afrique-occidentale, Westafrikanischer brauner Guereza.

Serval, *Felis serval,* chat tigre – Servalkatze.

And birds.

Flycatcher, red-bellied, *Tersiphone rufiventer,* Moucherolle à ventre roux – Waldparadiesschnäpper.

Heron, black, *Egretta ardesiaca,* héron noir – Glockenreiher.

Heron, night, *Nycticorax nycticorax,* héron bihoreau – Nachtreiher.

Jacana (lily-trotter), *Actophilornis africana,* jacana – Blaustirn Blatthünchen.

Kingfisher, giant, *Ceryle maxima,* martin-pêcheur géant – Riesenfischer.

Plover, spur-winged, *Vanellus spinosus,* vanneau armé – Spornkiebitz.

Starling, amethyst, *Cinnyricinclus leucogaster,* merle améthyste – Amethystglanzstar.

Touraco, violet, *Musophaga violacea,* Touraco violet – Schildturako.

Extinct. Since the white man came, The Gambia has lost many of its wild inhabitants. The last giraffe died near MacCarthy Island in 1899; the elephant has gone, and so have the buffalo, waterbuck, eland and hartebeest. Lions are extremely rare outside the Abuko Reserve, and leopards even rarer.

The white man is not entirely to blame, for during my first visit to the country I heard from separate sources of the man from Soma who shot a leopard in the bush. One story came from Europeans who heard the shot; the other came from Africans who saw him carrying the skin home on his shoulder.

Big game. You will hear rumours about big game, but you must get away from the main road if you are to see any. Hippos and crocodiles breed in the creeks by Pappa Island, and a rare hippo has been seen near Fatoto. For years I have heard stories of the enormous python which lives near Fatoto, and which – luckily – nobody will kill because it is the Devil incarnate. More recently another giant python has been seen several times near Denton Bridge, and traffic stops to let it cross the road: this particular serpent survives because it is sacred.

Snakes. There are probably around 30 species of snake in The Gambia, but only four of them are venomous. They *all* rush for the safety of cover at the approach of large creatures such as man, and none will attack anything too large for it to eat. As a full-grown adult is far too big for the largest python to swallow, you need have no fear whatever of snakes.

But you should be cautious when walking in tall grass or dense undergrowth, preferably by making a little noise to announce your coming, and giving any snake the chance to escape, for it may attack if cornered or forced to defend itself.

Your chances of seeing a snake are very remote. After spending months in east, west and north Africa, I have seen only one in the wild – a four-foot-or-so specimen in Bijilo Forest, The Gambia. It vanished within a second.

Buckle Street, Banjul; the city will take several years to complete its roadbuilding programme.

Primates. The most common mammalian wildlife is the monkeys, whom you will see on any up-country journey running across the road or looking at you from the treetops. The Gambia has the vervet, the western red colobus, the red patas and the rare mona monkey. Some of the tourist hotels have a semi-domesticated primate on the premises, but wild members of the species even cross the Denton Bridge and approach Banjul. Baboons are less venturesome, their troupes preferring the deeper bush to the east of Soma.

Crocodiles Many tourists see at least two crocodiles during their stay in The Gambia, not so much because these reptiles are common — they are not — but because they live in the Abuko Reserve and in the sacred crocodile pits in Bakau, at Kartung on the southern shore, and at Berending near Barra. These creatures' sacred existence comes from the ancient belief that they could cure infertility in women and bad luck in business for men. They could also bring a nasty death.

Three species of crocodile live in the Gambia River; the Nile croc, the bottle-nosed and the pygmy, the former growing up to 15 feet long; although they are not common, their presence is yet another reason why you shouldn't swim in the river.

Aardvark to warthog. You have even less chance of seeing several other species, either because they are rare or because of their shy or noctournal habits. Aardvarks, the 'earth pigs' of the Afrikaner, come out only at night to dine on termites; mongooses hunt mice and small birds by day and only rarely kill snakes; jackals and spotted hyenas

Fish-drying frames at Ghana Town. The village's inhabitants originated in Ghana.

announce themselves vocally; and fruit bats fly by night and are seen only briefly at dawn and dusk if you know exactly where to look.

The vast herds of grazing animals of eastern Africa are represented in the west of the continent by small numbers of small antelope including the oribi and the duiker, and the splayed-hoofed sitatunga which thrives in the swamps. Apart from the rare big cats, the felines are confined to the small and secretive civet and serval, and the unrelated genet.

And the warthog? There are sufficient of these ugly creatures for them to appear regularly on the Tendaba Camp menu, but they are secretive.

Water creatures. Sand crabs and fiddler crabs, the males of the latter each with one overgrown claw, thrive on the black beaches north of Barra, and mud oysters are in great numbers in the bolongs south of Banjul, their shells the source of local building lime, while the cockles from the mudflats have supplied sufficient shells to build the tarmac road to Soma. Along the river you may be fortunate enough to see an occcasional mudskipper, the fish that uses its fins to move over the mud and climb the mangrove roots, but you must come in the rainy season to see the lungfish.

Flora. The Gambia's flora contains some trees which make splendid isolated specimens, most noticeably the baobab, otherwise known as the bottle tree or the upside-down tree, from the old story that its branches are underground and its roots in the air as a divine

You can recognise a mahogany tree by its buttress-like roots. This specimen is in the Casamance, Senegal.

punishment for refusing to stay in one place.

The baobab normally sheds its leaves towards the end of the dry season but its seed pods, almost the size of small coconuts, linger. These pods contain a white powder which is the raw material for tartaric acid, and thus sherbert and similar sweets; Gambian children chew it in lumps until it turns red and unpalatable — rather like the kola nut which you'll find children selling from trays in every village. The bark of the baobab, by the way, produces a tough fibre, and many trees carry nasty scars around their base showing where they have been skinned.

The kapok or cottonsilk tree is another giant, its sweet-pea-sized seeds lying in the centre of a ball of down the size of a goose-egg. This silky down was used to fill mattresses and cushions until the coming of synthetic fibes and foam plastics. The mango tree forms an enormous, wide-spreading canopy covered in dark-green leaves during the tourist season, with its pear-sized fruits gradually ripening.

Any village that has had time to establish itself will have one of these three arboreal giants at its centre, and in the tree's shade, the *bantaba* or 'meeting place,' the village elders meet for their discussions, which have also taken the same name.

Bamboo grows to great heights in moist areas and provides the raw material for the walls of many of the village compounds, either standing alone or forming a skeleton which is then covered with mud. Elephant grass makes the roof, and the result is much more attractive than the corrugated iron compound which is insufferably hot in the early afternoon, and noisy during the rainy season.

Bamboo was also one of the raw materials for making charcoal, which is now totally banned in The Gambia and several other African countries: tiny Gambia has lost a third of its natural bush since independence, either to the charcoal burner or to the slash-and-burn farmer. Firing the bush is now an offence, but it still happens all too frequently, and there are not enough groundnut bricks, made from the harvest's waste products, to meet the demand for fuel. And bricks cost money, which is also in short supply.

11: THE NATION'S STORY

Wassu and the Empires to Senegambia

THE HISTORY OF THE GAMBIA began around 700AD when an unknown people from an unknown region built a series of stone circles, a mini-multi-Stonehenge, for reasons we still do not understand.

Wassu Stone Circles. Each of the sites, at Wassu and other places on the north bank as well as elsewhere in west Africa, has a collection of circles; those at Wassu must contain 60 to 80 rust-red laterite pillars from four to eight feet tall, but it's impossible to say how many circles there are as they merge into each other. The circles have no obvious use, certainly not for any solar observations nor as foundations for buildings, but the discovery of human remains buried around them suggests some kind of cemetery.

Laterite is a strange rock, the only hard stone found in The Gambia. Peculiar to the tropics, it is created by the action of sun and rain on the native soil and results in rough sandy stone with a high concentration of iron oxides. The name comes from the Latin *later*, 'brick.'

Sudan. Strangely, at the time the Wassu circles were being built (according to radio-carbon dating), the first Arab traders were crossing the Sahara from north to south with their camel trains. They thought of the desert as an ocean and called the fertile land beyond it, *sahel*, meaning 'shore,' though to us today the name conjures a fragile area of semi-desert and scrub. The country was *Bilad-al-Sudan*, the 'land of the blacks,' a name which has also changed its meaning, for 'Sudan' is now the specific nation of which Khartoum is the capital. But our Latin-origin words *Niger* and *Nigeria* still retain that meaning of blackness.

The Romans had called the coast around Carthage in Tunisia, *Ifriqya*, from which comes our 'Africa,' but it was the Arabs who brought to Europe the first news of the vast continent of Africa.

Kingdoms and empires. In response to these travellers from the north, the black peoples of the Sudan began forming themselves into kingdoms; in the 11th cent the Kingdom of Ghana occupied the territories we know today as western Mali and southern Mauritania; the name was to linger on in folk memory and in this century to be applied to the colony of the Gold Coast when it achieved independence.

Gold. There was plenty of gold in the region in those olden days. The blacks had no use for it, but when they found the Arabs lusted after the metal they gathered it from around the Senegal River and traded it, weight for weight, for salt.

The Almoravid Berbers defeated King Kanissai of Ghana and imposed Islam on his black peoples, but the creed of the Prophet had to accommodate strong tribal traditions and was inevitably less doctrinal here than in the Mediterranean lands.

Mali. The Kingdom, or Empire, of Mali, emerged in the 14th cent, incorporating today's Senegambia and most of Mali, which explains why this latter sector of the former French Sudan took this historic name when it achieved independence in modern times.

The Mali of old was centred on the new city of Timbuktoo and in 1324 King Mansa Musa of Mali left his palace in Timbuktoo on pilgrimage to Mecca, taking 500 slaves and 100 camels laden with gold, an incredible achievement for what is now one of the poorest countries in the world. But the old Mali was so wealthy — reckoned in gold if not in the produce of the land — that in the 15th cent internal strife shattered the empire, and the small Kingdom of the Songhai gradually emerged to take its place.

Songhai. The Songhai, centred on what we call Mali and Niger and with its capital at Gao, developed trade links with the Berbers in the 16th cent, but was unable to foresee events on a world scale. The Christians had driven the Moslems out of Spain and were sailing their little wooden ships across the Atlantic, along the Mediterranean, and down the coast of Africa, looking for the ocean route to the Spice Islands. They found, among other things, the trade route to West Africa.

Meanwhile, the Berbers were needed at home and they abandoned the overland route across the Sahara with the twin results that several of the vital oases were lost forever, and the Kingdom of the Songhai collapsed, leaving only its name to be corrupted down the ages into 'Senegal' and the family name 'Njie.' The European invaders and explorers were to find west Africa south of the Sahara an area of individual tribes, easy to conquer.

Slavery. The Africans had long ago realised their Berber customers were ready to trade in living human flesh. Warring tribes had earlier killed their enemies rather than take prisoners, but this demand for black flesh gave a commercial value to the warriors of the defeated tribes. At first the price was low — three slaves for a camel, and 25 slaves for a civet cat, although this creature lived wild in west Africa.

But the value of a black slave increased fivefold once his Berber owner delivered him to the markets of the Maghreb (*See 'Discover Tunisia' in this series*), and soon the merchants were paying higher prices down in the Sahel. If there were not enough prisoners from tribal wars to meet this growing demand, the black chiefs rounded up their own people and fathers sold their children into a lifetime of slavery.

The old slave house in Georgetown is now falling down.

Prester John. The Europeans, who weren't averse to taking Turks and Berbers into servitude, moved in to west Africa and realised that here was a cornucopia of black slaves all ready for loading aboard ship. In 1455 the Portuguese, inspired by their stay-at-home explorer Prince Henry the Navigator, sailed up the Gambia River but were deterred by the sight of the native canoes. They came back in 1456 and established a trading post on what they called Ilha de San André, since they had buried a sailor named André on the island; we know it as Fort James Island. They also gave the name of Cabo de Santa María to the headland we know as Cape Point in Bakau.

John Hawkins. The Portuguese were not interested in slavery at this stage, concentrating instead on the search for the legendary lands of Prester John. But in 1510 the first slaver left the Dark Continent for Hispaniola, and in 1562 John Hawkins captained England's first slave ship to sail from west Africa.

From that first shipment in 1510, to 1856 when the United States abolished slavery, 12,000,000 blacks left west Africa for the New World, according to one estimate, and in the peak period from 1680 to 1700, according to another estimate, 300,000 blacks went from Africa to the West Indies and North America. But nobody was counting: the supply was inexhaustible, and if an English trader was becalmed in the Doldrums the crew threw the slaves overboard before they died of starvation. The French were arguably more humane: if famine threatened, they would poison a chunk of their human cargo. Dr David

Livingstone guessed that 90% of the slaves died on the Atlantic crossing, but Alex Haley in *Roots* suggests the success rate was much higher, and common sense would support him.

Fort James Island. The Duke of Courland, a nobleman of Hansa (German) origins, built a fort on the former Portuguese Ilha de San André in 1651. From this base he negotiated with the King of Niumi who lived on the north shore, buying slaves for his sugar plantations on the Caribbean island of Tobago. Although Courland's title suggested ancestry in what we know as Latvia and Lithuania, he preferred the tropics and enjoyed a regal lifestyle.

Ten years later the 'Royal Adventurers of England Trading into Africa' seized Ilha de San André and renamed it Fort James Island, from the man who was to become King James II of England in 1685.

Dog Island. The British even occupied Dog Island for a few years, abandoning it in 1666. The isle took its name from the barking, dog-like baboons that menaced the first settlers. You can reach the island on foot at low tide, but you will find nothing of the Fort Charles which was built here in the brief years of occupation when the place gloried under the name of Charles Island.

Albreda. The French were already active in west Africa though they had yet to make any impact on the north of the continent. In 1681 they came into the Gambia River and followed Courland's example by leasing a tiny parcel of land on the north shore from the King of Niumi, paying an annual rental of four bars of iron. Here they set up the trading post of Albadar, soon to be corrupted to Albreda, and here they stayed resolutely until 1857, ultimately a mini French enclave in a tiny English colony in the larger French colony of Senegal.

England was so weak in the area it had no option but to acknowledge French ownership of Albreda. Fire destroyed the settlement in 1686, and in 1689 when the English managed to seize the rebuilt fort they declared their intention of defending it to the death. Six years later, French reinforcements demanded the English surrender, toasted the health of King William III, fired two shots — and the English garrison duly gave itself up. The French then turned their attention to Fort James, seized the island, flattened the fort's masonry and spiked the guns. And then *they* withdrew.

Freedom flagpole. During Albreda's subsequent history as a slave-loading base, its French contingent was often down to two people whose sole duty was to raise the tricolour at dawn on Sunday and lower it at sunset. This flagpole became of great significance to the black population when Britain abolished slavery, for any slave who managed to escape and reach the pole was given his freedom. Sadly, this piece of history has been lost and in its place is an 18-pound cannon made in 1810.

The Royal African Company rebuilt Fort James, but the French seized it yet again in 1702 and demanded a ransom of £6,000. The English agreed, but regretted that they could pay only in instalments of £2,000. Meanwhile, they rebuilt the fort and manned it with the castouts of London society, and it was these men who mutinied in 1708, spiked the guns, and managed to find a passage home.

Piracy. The Treaty of Utrecht in 1713 left conditions in limbo — except that Britain now had control of Gibraltar, a staging-post on the west Africa run — and in 1719 a British privateer, Hywel Davis, seized the fort on James Island which had been rebuilt yet again. He plundered the stores and recruited half the 14-man garrison before sailing off to other adventures. On All Saints Day 1725, the powder magazine on Fort James Island exploded, once more demolishing most of the fortress, but the British painstakingly rebuilt it, for the French were still across the water in Albreda.

Senegambia. The Seven Years' War ended with the signing of the Treaty of Paris in 1763 giving, among other transfers, Louisiana to Spain and Canada and Senegal (except Gorée Island by Dakar) to Britain. But the French stayed on in Albreda.

Colonel O'Hara. The Governor of this new colony of Senegambia based himself in St Louis, on the mouth of the Senegal River, and appointed Colonel O'Hara of the Coldstream Guards his lieutenant-governor in The Gambia. The colonel settled on Fort James Island — this was, after all, the only fortress the British yet had in The Gambia — and called for reinforcements.

Tribal dancing tourist-style. This demonstration was at the Tropic Gardens Hotel.

And this ties in very nicely with Alex Haley's research into his *Roots*, as he could place 'the coming of the king's soldiers' to 1767 and so fix the year in which his ancestor Kinta Kunde was taken into slavery.

The Gambia is British. But O'Hara's reinforcements were a rabble, barely able to withstand an attack in 1768 by 500 warriors from the King of Niumi. In 1779 the French were more successful and managed to sack Fort James for the umpteenth time — and this time it stayed derelict, as you see it today. The American War of Independence and its resulting Treaty of Versailles, in January 1783, gave Senegal back to the French and confirmed British rule in The Gambia. But did Britain *want* this latest colony?

Wilberforce and Clarkson. Events in Britain were dictating the future for all of Black Africa. In 1759, William Wilberforce was born in Hull, son of the landed gentry; and in 1760, Thomas Clarkson was born in Wisbech, son of the headmaster of my former Grammar School. Clarkson took up the anti-slavery cause in 1785 and became vice-president of the Anti-Slavery Society, working with Wilberforce who joined the cause in 1788 and used his office as MP for Hull to help bring in the Act which abolished slavery in British territories in 1808; it's gratifying to see that both men are remembered in Banjul street names.

Mungo Park. Mungo Park was born in Foulshiels, Selkirkshire, in 1771, the son of a farmer. He qualified as a doctor of medicine at Edinburgh in 1792 then spent a year as surgeon on a ship sailing to Sumatra. With the wanderlust in his soul he applied to the Association for Promoting the Discovery of the Inland Parts of the Continent of Africa, happily known for short as the African Association, and in June 1795 he landed at Jillifree, today's Juffure, with the task of going inland to find the source of the Niger and, if possible, to be the first white man to visit legendary Timbuctoo.

Mumbo-jumbo. With his travelling companions, a freed Jamaican slave called Johnson, and a Gambian known as Demba, Park plunged eastward. Near Tambacounda in Senegal he found a mask and cloak, made from baobab fibre and other tree bark, hanging on a branch. His companions explained that this was the mama-jumbo mask which a man, or his friend, would wear to settle an argument between his wives, or to drive away the spirits of the ancestors.

The mama-jumbo would call for a village meeting with singing and dancing then, when night had fallen, he would point out his victim: the wife who talked too much or who backanswered; or the person possessed by the ancestral ghosts. The victim would be stripped, bound to a post, and flogged. Later explorers failed to understand the significance of the act and so 'mumbo-jumbo' has come into the language meaning senseless talk.

Park moved on, trying to evade the Berbers who had recrossed the Sahara and were occupying Timbuctoo, but they caught him and threatened him with death or having his eyes put out. He escaped after two months and, now travelling alone and by night, reached the Niger River but had to turn back after a year on the trail.

There was famine in the Mandinka lands, but he managed to survive by joining a slave merchant trekking to the Gambia River which he reached in April of 1797. He was home just before Christmas to report on his adventures.

Park memorial. Back in The Gambia in 1804 for a second attempt on the source of the Niger, he sailed upriver to near Karantaba Tenda and then struck off inland: a small obelisk on the river bank marks the spot where he landed. He reached the Niger, though he never lived to find its source nor tread the streets of mystic Timbuctoo, for he made one fatal mistake. He forgot to give 'dash' — a bribe, or a token of goodwill — to a chief whose territory he wanted to cross, and he paid with his life.

Sierra Leone. From 1783 Britain owned The Gambia — but the little colony's boundaries were still to be decided, and the only colonial settlement in British hands was the tiny Fort James, now derelict. In 1807, the year that it abolished slavery, Britain handed The Gambia to the governor of Sierra Leone, who was to run both territories as one while the new colonial masters looked for another use for the Gambia River.

Colonel Charles MacCarthy, governor-in-chief of Britain's West African Territories, wanted control of James Island in order to enforce the ban on slavery, which was still going on in The Gambia. He sent in Captain Alexander Grant to resettle the island, but Grant's comment was that Fort James was too small, too isolated, and too far upstream to be effective, although the British moved in to occupy the ruined fort in 1814.

Kombo St Mary. MacCarthy decided that the flat and uninhabited marshy island at the mouth of the river would be a better site for settlement, so on 23 April 1816 the British leased it from the chieftain of the Kombo, the higher land to the south. Remembering the name Cabo de Santa María the Portuguese had given to a nearby headland, the British in their inventiveness called this St Mary's Island, the name it still carries today. The administrative district has taken the name of Kombo St Mary, a happy marriage of black and white cultures.

Bathurst. The settlement that grew up on St Mary's Island took its name from Henry, the third Earl of Bathurst, who was Secretary for War and the Colonies from 1815 to 1827 and a disciple of Pitt the Younger. But when a European asked an African what he was searching for in a clump of bamboo on St Mary's Island, he was told, in Mandinka, 'fibre for making a seat.' The Mandinka word for 'seat' is *ban,* and 'fibre' is *jul,* according to this legend, and if the story is true it would appear the name Banjul is as old as the city itself.

The round house at Toniataba is supposedly The Gambia's largest African-style building.

Georgetown. In 1823 the British went upstream and leased the island of Jangjangbure from the King of Kolli, renaming it first Lemain and then from Colonel MacCarthy. Georgetown was named either from George III or George IV; more important is that the little community was Britain's first upriver attempt at colonial administration in The Gambia and not, as one Gambian lad told me, "the first place upriver to be civilized." He forgot the empires of the Mali and the Songhai.

Fort Bullen. The British, realising they needed extra armaments on the north shore, wanted to build a fort by Barra but had to wait until 1823 and a new King of Niumi, who demanded £100 a year for the concession. Commodore Bullen, a veteran of Trafalgar and commanding officer of HMS *Maidstone*, which ferried the first two cannon across to the new fort, supervised the building and gave the bastion his name.

Barra War. This new King of Niumi, Burungay, was soon abusing British traders in Barra to such an extent that his income was suspended. This led to a drunken brawl which would have been a skirmish in a larger country, but which in tiny Gambia has gone into history as the Barra War of 1827, and there is a plaque in St Mary's Cathedral, Banjul, commemorating one of its European victims.

Cannons. Strangely, the French helped the British finish the fort in 1831. Fort Bullen from then on never fired a shot in anger, and its cannon now lie scattered across the headland, gradually rusting back into the red earth. To complement the Fort Bullen artillery, a battery of six 24-pound cannon was located at Bathurst on the headland where Sir Dawda Jawara was later to have his presidential palace, and there were (and still are) others at Batelling near Tendaba Camp. In 1857 the British inherited the guns at Albreda when the French pulled out, and there's also a stray cannon outside the Atlantic Hotel, but nobody knows its origins.

The colonial engineer and town planner, Mr Buckle, decided that Bathurst town should radiate from Macarthy Square at its centre, and with the Battle of Waterloo (1815) still in mind he had little difficulty in naming the roads that were to surround Buckle Street: Wellington, of course, and then each of the general's aides was remembered: Blücher, Picton, Anglesea (but the street is named *Anglesey*), Hill, Cotton, and the Prince of Orange (from whom Orange Street takes its name). Plus, of course, Clarkson and Wilberforce.

Blücher Street became Cameron Street during the First World War, and the original Wilberforce Street gave way to Independence Drive.

Churches. The Wesleyan Church was built on Dobson Street in 1835, replacing the one burned down by its congregation in 1822 when the preacher asked them to discard their lucky charms, their *jujus*. In the following year the Anglican Bishop of Sierra Leone responded to merchants' requests by sending a priest to Bathurst, though this preacher also had to start his ministry without a church or cathedral: the finishing touches to St Mary's Anglican Cathedral came in 1901.

Crown colony. By 1843 The Gambia was sufficiently important to be removed from the control of Sierra Leone and become a crown colony, but in 1866 it was relegated to the West African Settlements.

River steamers. The British had already realised that the essence of the colony of The Gambia was its river. The first steamer service had started in 1830 with the *Wilberforce*, strictly on Government service and not for passengers, native or otherwise. The *Albert* followed, but she was lost in 1841. Then came the *Dover,* abandoned in 1866 when Britain offered The Gambia to France, which declined, being more concerned with problems in Germany and Austria.

Lady Chilel. With the resumption of services came the *St Mary,* the *Vampire,* several boats bearing the name *Mansa Kila,* and in 1922 the first passenger steamer, the *Prince of Wales.* To bring this riverine saga up to date, the *Lady Denham* followed in 1929 and the *Lady Wright* in 1951.

When this second lady of the river needed to be pensioned off in the 1970s, President Jawara played his political hand. Shortly after the Chileans had cancelled an order for British gunboats, the Gambian president approached Judith Hart, the Minister for Overseas Development in the Labour Government and the MP for the shipbuilding constituency of Lanark, The Gambia got its replacement, the £1,500,000 *Lady Chilel Jawara,* which was launched in March 1978. It sank in the mid-1980s with some loss of life.

Post Office. Back in the 1850s The Gambia was ready to follow the example of Rowland Hill's 'universal penny post,' started in Britain in 1840. Previously, the only means of sending letters to Europe was to forward them to Freetown with money to cover the postage from there, and trust to luck; return mail had to come by the same perilous route. But in 1858 the one-man Bathurst Post Office opened for business, with the first Gambian stamps going on issue in 1869.

Soniki-Marabout War. Another series of skirmishes from the 1850s to the '70s has been raised to the status of a war, the Soniki-Marabout War. Moslems from Senegal led Serahuli and Jola warriors on raids into The Gambia, destroying Brikama in 1854 and again in 1874. At one stage, around 200 women and children fled to Dog Island for safety.

Boundaries. In 1884 Otto Leopold, the Prince of Bismarck-Schönhausen, called a conference of Europe's colonial powers to divide the continent of Africa among themselves. France owned the largest chunk, from Brazzaville on the Congo to Tunis, and from Dakar east through 35 degrees of longitude to the edge of the Nile basin.

Within that mass there were no individual boundaries; Senegal and French Guinea were undefined areas. The British, now keen to hold onto The Gambia, raised St Mary's Island and Bathurst to the status of a Crown colony in December 1888 with its Legislative Council reintroduced, though the remainder of the territory, still without fixed boundaries, became a protectorate. Starting in 1890 Britain began defining the frontiers of The Gambia, beginning with the lines of latitude at 13° 12' 15'' North and 13° 32' 56'' North, totally arbitrary markings on the map, as were so many of Africa's frontiers.

The great northward sweep of the river by Kaur put a stop to that simple method so Britain and France compromised by agreeing on a boundary that marked the effective range of fire of a gunboat. Gradually the curving frontier was agreed, reaching up the Gambia River to the limits of navigation, the Falls of Barrakunda beyond Fatoto.

With the frontier fixed, the administrators could go to work. In 1906 the protectorate was split into five divisions, which are virtually unaltered to this day except for changes of name: Kombo-Foni became Western Division and South Bank became Lower River, leaving the North Bank, Macarthy Island and Upper River divisions as they were. Within the divisions there are 36 districts, each ruled by an elected chief.

War. The First World War never touched The Gambia, and the Second one affected the colony and protectorate only because aircraft could fly much further. The Public Works Department built enormous hangars — using corrugated iron, of course — at the southern tip of town, where Sunderland flying boats were based for their patrols far out into the Atlantic. Elsewhere, airstrips were carved in the bush at Tendaba, and at Yundum to replace the strip at Jeshwang (Serekunda).

Groundnuts. After the war, Britain's Labour Government tried to stimulate the Gambian economy by boosting the production of the groundnut, peanut or monkey nut, *arachis hypogaea,* an annual plant of the *leguminosae* order which originated in South America. The Portuguese had brought the nut from Brazil in the 16th cent, and in 1854 Louis Faidherbe, Governor of Dakar, had grown groundnuts for cash, and they were already part of the west Africans' daily diet.

The Gambian Groundnuts Scheme was only a partial success from a British viewpoint, but the nuts are now vital to the Gambians who grew 128,000 tons of them in 1982-3, shipping the best peanut oil to Britain in bulk, making soap with the poorer grade oil, and pressing the husks into fuel for the cooking fires of the compounds.

Independence. Throughout the world, colonies were now demanding independence, and on 4 October 1963 The Gambia started to govern itself as preparation for its independence on 8 February 1965. The little country remains in the Commonwealth but on 24 April 1970 it declared itself the Republic of The Gambia. And in 1973 Bathurst changed its name to Banjul — but there are no plans to drop Macarthy for Janjangbure nor to find alternatives for Georgetown or James Island. "Historical associations," I was told, a reminder that the Gambians are proud of their links with Great Britain.

Senegambia. The story doesn't end there, for The Gambia and big brother Senegal, which would have been one country but for European intervention, turned their thoughts to achieving that dream as the Republic of Senegambia. Both countries signed a Treaty of Association in 1967, and they began moving slowly towards a union, but on 30 September 1989 the federation split because Senegal considered The Gambia was moving too slowly.

The problem was that the Gambians have become proud of their little nation, poor though it may be, and they are happy with the legacies of British colonialism. They may be ethnically the same people as the Senegalese, but they don't like the Senegalese way of doing things, and they decided to keep their independence.

12: SIGHTSEEING IN THE GAMBIA

A slice of colonial history

BANJUL IS A CHARMING CITY beneath its layers of Harmattan dust. The size of an average small town in Europe, it retains the atmosphere of being an outpost of empire in the 1930s, and Gambians still play the occasional game of cricket on the Victoria Recreation Ground which takes up the centre of MacCarthy Square.

War memorial. On the south-east of the square stands the country's main war memorial, recalling the names of 38 members of the Royal West Africa Frontier Forces (The Gambia Company) who died in the Great War of 1914-18. The other war memorial is on New Town Rd, Fajara.

Albert Market. A long, low wall on the north-east side of Russell Street has small openings that lead through into one of Banjul's tourist sights, the Albert Market. This is a true African market with no concession to Europeans, where traders occupy tiny wooden stalls and sell pots and pans, enamel bowls, battery radios, dried herbs, and a wide range of toiletries from Europe. The market was burned down in the 1980s and in 1992-93 was rebuilt with help from China.

Naafi. Beyond the GPO, Wellington Street leads past the Customs and Excise and the Law Courts, past the ultra-modern BICI building and the CFAO supermarket to Anglesey Street where the vast Naafi (Navy, Army and Air Force Institute) building is now the Banjul National Shipping Agency and Bou Sleyman's hardware store, but still looks as if it belongs to an army camp.

Half Die. Beyond the Barra ferry terminal, Wellington Street enters the poorer parts of town, swings into tiny Wilberforce Street, unworthy of its namesake, — and into the Half Die, a district of corrugated iron compounds with open drainage whose name recalls the cholera epidemic of 1869. More than a century later the Half Die's drainage problem has still to be solved.

Sunderland hangars. From the bus station on Cotton Street, Bund Road leads out on a flood-prevention dyke across the mangrove swamps, with the sea on the left and the enclosed waters of the Crab Island ponding area on the right. It's a wonderful place to see the bird life, and until 1989 you could look back at the vast corrugated-iron hangars that held Sunderland flying boats which went on convoy protection and anti-submarine patrols during the Second World War.

Anti-aircraft. Or you can come up Dobson Street, past the sand-covered King George V Memorial Park, where almost 100 anti-aircraft guns were sited during the war. Although Senegal was occupied by Vichy France, there was never any threat to The Gambia and the guns never fired in anger.

Catholic Cathedral. Coming north along Dobson Street you will see the Catholic Cathedral fronting onto Picton Street, but with its entrance on Hagan, through a courtyard. This cathedral is much bigger than the Anglican one, and more impressive, with a wood-lined domed ceiling over the high altar, and a wood-lined barrel-shaped ceiling over the nave, though with corrugated iron on the outside. The upper parts of the windows have large red discs reminiscent of the sun, and there is seating for several hundred people.

Methodist Bookshop. The Gambia's only proper bookshop is in the former Methodist Girls' High School on Buckle St. An English missionary opened a shop to sell magazines, and the business just grew.

Box Bar. At the top of Dobson Street, Gamtel's technical depot faces the entrance to Uncle Joe's Guest House and Clarkson Street. From here, two distinctly different routes beckon: to the west, Lasso Wharf leads to Imam Omar Sowe Avenue and the quaintly named Box Bar Road, which recalls the 'box bar' or sluice gate built in 1862 to help drain the many streets that were regularly flooded at high tide; records claim that people have caught fish in the streets, and several crocodiles have wandered into town.

Imam Omar Sowe. Omar Sowe was an *imam* — a holy man — who saw Banjul threatened by a high tide in 1947. He stood on the roadway fronting onto the Crab Island mudflats and told the tide to go back. It did, and the imam was thereafter credited with supernatural powers. Soon after, King George IV agreed to a petition and the roadway was given its present name, Imam Omar Sowe Ave.

State House. Or go to the east, past MacCarthy Square again and to the cluster of smart government offices and the Government Printer. A path leads out by the Six-Gun Battery with its 24-pounders, and in two minutes you can be on the beach; or you may come down the northern side of MacCarthy Square, passing the Quadrangle which holds more government offices and which masks the off-limits State House in its own grounds.

St Mary's Cathedral. Ahead lies the Anglican Cathedral of St Mary, slumbering under its corrugated iron roof beside the square and looking no bigger than a parish church in some small English village.

It's just as homely, but the wall plaques remind you that this is not England, but colonial Africa in the days of the pith helmet and the puttee:

Lt John Hamilton, RN, age 18, slain 21 February 1861 while storming a stockade at the Battle of Saba...

Captain H T M Cooper, RM, acting administrator of Her Majesty's Settlement on The Gambia, died 9 January 1877...

Sacred to the memory of Edward Francis Foster, aged 38, who received his home call on the morning of 30 September 1918...

National Museum. Turn right into Gloucester Street, pass the depot for tourist taxis and bush taxis, still labelled *for hackney carriages only,* and you find the National Museum in your right in the former British Council building, reopened in 1982 as The Gambia's only true museum.

For D5, and a further D10 to use your camera, you have a very good insight into the tribal, colonial, and post-independence history of the region in a well-presented setting. Among the displays are dolls and symbolic dolls that infertile Jola and Mandinka women carried as substitutes for the children they could not have.

The tribespeople lived in harmony with nature, and the cycle of birth and death; when a mother lost one of her newly-born twins, she would replace it with a doll which had to be dressed and caressed daily, with its surviving sibling.

Mandinka circumcision masks, wickerwork baskets, looms, pottery, royal drums, pre-colonial iron cooking pots, tribal weapons, and early firearms: they all have a place here. There's also a good collection of relics of the slave trade, and of early photographs of Banjul — including one of the 1948 flood which Imam Omar Sowe did not stop.

Sam Jack. At the International Fast Food Cafe, Sam Jack Terrace leads away to the left; this street commemorates a Speaker in the National Assembly. But Independence Drive also starts here, running parallel to Marine Parade and holding the heart of The Gambia: the United Nations building, the Royal Victoria Hospital, the Banjul City Council and the unimposing National Assembly itself, with the Atlantic Hotel beyond.

Great Mosque. Midway along this stretch of Independence Drive stands a smallish mosque which until recently went under the name of the Great Mosque. The first mosque on this site, in the 1870s, was made of grass; this 1930s replacement is of breeze block, but the new Great Mosque, a truly impressive building, was completed in 1988 at the *other* end of the nearby Mosque Road, occupying what was the football stadium.

Skeletons. The coast between the outskirts of Banjul and the Wadner Beach Hotel is being eroded, with the bizarre result that human bones and the occasional complete skeleton are washed out of

Denton Bridge. A little more than two miles out of town is The Gambia's ultimate in impressive structures: the latest Denton Bridge. The first crossing of Oyster Creek was by oared ferry, then by a small paddle-boat. Building of the first bridge began in 1879 and was completed in 1885; within the decade it had been named from Governor Denton.

The present bridge was built between May 1984 and August 1986 by Keir International at a cost of £2,750,000 provided by the Overseas Development Corporation. It is 690 feet (210 metres) long, consisting of 13 spans each of 16m; beneath these are 84 steel tube piles weighing 740 tons and going 130 feet (40 metres) into the ground, and above them are 91 beams each weighing 11 tons, supporting a concrete deck capable of carrying a dual-carriageway.

UP-COUNTRY

BAKAU

Bakau, 'big place,' is a community at two levels, the majority of the Africans there to serve the Europeans in the coastal hotels. At the top level you will see some of The Gambia's best domestic architecture with the British High Commissioner's Residence, Dr Sir Dawda Jawara's Presidential Palace (you'll often see his motorcade going through the village), the expatriates' smart homes, and the hotels.

At the bottom level conditions are not so pleasant, and my unverified information is that some of the Gambians pay a weekly rental of D70 for these compounds. Put your cameras away, wander down the backalleys, and you will quickly understand many things, notably why there are so many self-appointed tourist guides and why Action Aid and the other charities have much work to do in the country.

Crocodile pit. The Katchikali sacred-crocodile pit is on the edge of the African village, a man-made hollow around 200 feet across by maybe 20 deep, and with four or five resident reptiles. This is one of three such pits in The Gambia, the others being at Berending on the North Bank, and Kartung; childless women, and men with business worries come here to seek the answers to their problems. Admission to the enclosure is D10.

Wartime relics. St Peter's Church, on Atlantic Boulevard, began life as a World War Two hut for the Royal Army Medical Corps, but was rebuilt when the tourist boom began. The military cemetery on Pipeline Road, between Fajara and Serekunda, holds some 200 graves from The Gambia and other commonwealth countries, a few of which face Mecca.

A baobab by Serekunda market

SEREKUNDA

Kunda means 'the town of, the home of,' and Sere's home town of Serekunda is the biggest in The Gambia with around 10% of the total population. It's a bustling town with a busy market which almost encircles the country's busiest bush-taxi depot. There are two smart churches on the road to Banjul; Christ's Church has, like the Bakau church, graduated from a wartime hut. Don't be alarmed at the alternative names to the place: Sere Kunda, Serrekunda or Serakunda.

To the north-east in the suburb of Kanifing is the light industry of the country, mainly confined to assembly, packaging and bottling plants.

YUNDUM

Lufthansa flew down to Jeshwang airstrip near Serekunda before World War Two, but a 1939 crash which killed all 23 people in the plane brought services to an abrupt halt. The Royal Air Force opted for Yundum airstrip and laid two nearly-all-weather runways from sand-track, the steel sheets that trans-saharan truck drivers use on loose dunes. Balfour Beatty built the full-length runway which allowed B.Cal's jets into the country. Remarkably, Concorde has even made a call here and the extra-long runway is an emergency landing strip for the NASA space shuttle.

THE KOMBOS (SOUTH GAMBIA)

The moderate-sized village of **Brufut** has an impressive Moslem cemetery. Nearby **Ghana Town** has some large fish-smoking sheds and a series of drying-racks, with only a faint odour of fish.

Tanji has another series of smoking-sheds beside the road down to the beach; here you can buy smoked bonga for 50 bututs each. The beach here is wide at low tide, and several tour operators use it as a road to or from the tourist hotels, but rounding **Solifor Point,** the country's westernmost headland, can be difficult unless the tide is right out.

In the late 19th cent, several marabouts (holy men) lived at **Gunjur,** making the British administrators fearful of another rebellion similar to the Soninki-Marabout War, so as a precaution they destroyed the nearby village of Sabiji. Gunjur escaped punishment, and this busy market village is now the centre of an area with strong Moslem beliefs and associations.

THE SOUTH BANK TO SOMA

Brefet is the site of a trading station established in 1664 but destroyed by the French from Albreda, on the opposite bank, in 1724. The British rebuilt it but Albreda's slave traders again destroyed it in 1820. Clarkson and Wilberforce had managed to urge the abolition of slavery in Britain and its colonies by 1807, but the law was not enforceable in Albreda where the French still reigned supreme.

Bintang, on the Bintang Bolong, has one of the most beautiful river settings in The Gambia and is worth the detour for that alone. Further east, **Bwiam** is renowned for its mysterious iron pot. Half a mile south-east of the Catholic School this alleged 'cooking pot' of unknown vintage is half-buried, inverted, with its three stumpy legs visible. Legend claims it cannot be dug up, despite several attempts, and legend also claims that in pre-colonial times the pot had the ability to turn and indicate the direction of impending attack.

I can now explain it all. The 'pot' is probably the cemented-in base for a small gun, which would obviously be turned to face the enemy.

A collection of corrugated-iron shops marks **Kalaji,** where a police road check delays all African transport. A Fula from Senegal and a family from Guinea Bissau are the main traders. On the edge of the village is the single-track 380-foot-long bridge, built in 1962 across the Bintang Bolong.

At **Sankandi,** where two British colonial officers were killed in 1900, a poor track leads north-west to **Keneba,** one of the most isolated villages in the country. For this reason the Medical Research Council has been here since the sixties, studying malaria, bilharzia and other tropical

Is the legendary 'cooking pot' at Bwiam really the mounting for a piece of light artillery?

diseases. North, and on the river bank, is **Tankular,** which has a small ship's bell bearing the date 1711. The bell, used only as a general alarm, may have come from the Portuguese trading post which was a little way upstream.

Back on the main road is **Dumbutu** which the British destroyed in 1901, fearing an uprising after the killing of the two officers in Sankandi. **Kwinella,** the next roadside village, was a fierce battleground during the Soniki-Marabout War, with around 500 villagers and warriors being killed in 1863.

From each of these villages a track leads into the bush to **Batelling,** where four cannon are all that remain from an earlier trading station. A track leads to **Tendaba** which was the site of yet another trading post before the present camp was built. *Tenda* means 'quay' and *ba* means 'big,' so you can judge for yourself. *Nding,*, by the way, means 'small.'

Toniataba has an exceptionally large round-house, some 200 feet in circumference; dimensions are not exact as the place is almost continually being repaired, bit by bit. An earlier occupant was a Mandinka marabout, Sheikh Othman, whose name is of Turkish origins. He lived to a great age, well past 100 years, and is supposedly buried under the floor of what is now the private living-quarters of the present marabout who has been here 30 years and teaches local children the Koran. You may photograph him for a fee.

The Transgambia Highway is **Soma's** lifeblood. The village has a police and customs station, a petrol pump, a small hotel and a big market, and is a staging point for buses and bush taxis.

THE SOUTH BANK: SOMA TO FATOTO

Mansa Konko, 'chieftain's hill,' is the administrative centre of the Lower River Division. The choice of a site was a compromise to avoid offense to any of the four nearby villages which would have welcomed the rise in status. Of the four, **Pakali Nding,** 'small Pakali,' is now as large as Pakali Ba, 'big Pakali,' some way down the road.

Georgetown is one of those places you must visit. It was the second onshore colony in The Gambia and is one of the few African villages to have a European-inspired street plan based on the grid system.

The town is decaying slowly, now that the river traffic has given way to buses. The market has gone to Bansang and an air of fading colonialism hangs heavy, but the town is still the capital of the Macarthy Island Division, it has one of the country's two prisons — the British played with the idea of making the entire island a penal colony — and it has its celebrated school.

A century ago the 'Chiefs' School' was the only up-country place where village chiefs could have their sons educated. The school was expanded in 1927 and given the name of the Armitage High School, honouring the retiring governor, and it now takes 500 boarding pupils, including a few girls and a few pupils from other English-speaking west African nations. Charities help to maintain the school, and on an earlier visit I met the principal, Musa Sanneh, who showed me some of the hoes, rakes and even door-hinges made by hand in the school workshops.

'Enter to learn, go forth to serve,' says the motto over the main door, and nowadays all subjects are taught up to Ordinary Level; after that, Gambian pupils must continue their studies in Banjul or Brikama.

The slave house in Georgetown is the prime tourist attraction. Now roofless, its sturdy walls stand beside the ferry terminal as a reminder of mankind's inhumanity to man, black to black as well as white to black. Pace it out: I reckon it could have held up to 500 slaves at a moderate squeeze.

Across the tarmac road a more recent colonial building has a ramp at its far end leading down to a basement where other slaves were kept, while (according to legend) British army officers lived overhead. The cellar is now home to a number of large bats.

Bansang is a bustling community between the river and a rounded hill; climb it for a view of the countryside.

Sotuma and **Alohungari,** both on the new tarmac road leading into Basse, have potters who sell their wares in Basse itself; depending on your transport arrangements, you may be able to see the potters at work.

Basse Santa Su is at the end of the tarmac road. The village — or is it a town? — is the largest settlement east of Brikama and is the capital of the Upper River Division. It has two cinemas, two banks, a good secondary school which was founded in 1929, and an overflowing market.

The name is usually shortened to Basse, pronounced 'bassee,' as the *Santa Su* which means 'upper home' is the vibrant heart of the community. Basse Duma Su, 'lower home,' was down by the riverside and prone to flooding. Despite the demise of Duma Su, several of the large and crumbling colonial buildings there are occupied in the dry season.

The now-defunct Gambia Produce Marketing Board took over the peanut and cotton business in 1974 and ran the depots on each side of the river at Basse, where 5,600 tons of peanuts can be stored. The crop goes from here to Banjul by barge where most is processed for oil extraction at the factory near Denton Bridge.

If you are driving your own vehicle (not a hire car) and have the necessary paperwork, you can formally go through customs and immigration at Basse and head south to Sabi and on to Velingara in Senegal, for the road to the Niokolo Koba National Park.

A dusty track leads to **Fatoto** at the extreme east of The Gambia. The village has a small factory for cleaning, weighing and bagging groundnuts, and a large compound where the incoming nuts are stored. There is no loading jetty here, so the crop is hauled by tractor and trailer to Basse.

Fatoto's market is tiny and primitive, and the well beside it yields water that is green for lack of use, now the mains supply has arrived. There is a small primary school, a police station, a clinic, and a Gamtel office combined with the post office. There is no hotel, no bank, and mains water to only half the village, but the gentle pace of the people can teach Europeans the meaning of happiness. And the ferry is wonderfully photogenic.

At Fatoto you are very much aware of the long, long road back to Banjul, but just six miles to the south-east across the bush lies a good tarmac road in Senegal, and 30 miles (48km) across country to the north-east is Tambacounda, with a tarmac road, a railway and an airport.

Two miles from Fatoto is **Kristi Kunda,** 'Christ's home,' where Anglican missionaries established a boarding school at the turn of the century; a few boulders now mark the spot. The last priest in the village was the Very Rev J. C. Faye who in 1951 founded the Democratic Party; this Christian-inspired movement merged with a Moslem force to become the Democratic Congress Party and has since been absorbed by other parties.

And finally there are the elusive **Barrakunda Falls,** the head of navigation of the Gambia River. In 1989, travelling by car, I took a guide at Fatoto to Kristi Kunda and engaged another there to take us all to Koina, the last village. After driving through near-trackless bush, we reached the river. But no falls. Of course not: they're four miles (6km) further upstream, in Senegal.

THE NORTH BANK

The North Bank has less to offer, mainly because communications are so much more difficult. **Barra** has the derelict Fort Bullen and the peanut loading wharf, and **Berending** its crocodile pit, but the main feature of interest is in **Juffure and Albreda,** which you will almost certainly reach by river. The slave house is well-preserved, now surrounded by baobabs and without its freedom flagpole, but when you walk into Juffure compare the village with Alex Haley's account of the place — allowing for the the passage of centuries — and decide how much poetic license he has used.

Beyond **Kerewan,** which takes its name from the Tunisian holy city Kairouan, there is indeed a village called **Kinteh Kunda,** the name of that original Gambian ancestor who was taken into slavery. And north lies **Juwara** which was once the biggest town on the north bank. It has gone into sharp decline since independence.

Swamps on the Diabugo Bolong by Fatoto are popular with egrets.

The stone circles at Wassu; their origin is unknown.

Farafenni, like Soma, is a market and a staging point, but with a far better hotel.

When King Kolli ceded MacCarthy Island to the British in 1823, his neighbour Kemintang showed his disagreement by plundering the passing boat traffic. The Governor banned all boat movement upstream of Georgetown from 1834, which boosted Kemintang's confidence. By 1841 he had added Fula warriors to his troops and was threatening **Kantaba,** to the west. The chief of Kantaba asked the British for help, signed a pact with the Governor in Bathurst, and saw Kantaba Fort built. The garrison stayed only one year; Kemintang backed away and the presence of the fort, now in advanced decay, was sufficient to keep the peace.

The school at **Balanghar** used to receive help from tourists aboard the *Spirit of Galicia;* beyond it lies **Kaur,** sometimes called Kau-Ur, a busy village at the end of a spur road off the main dust road. There is a customs post, a reminder that Senegal is never far away, and the groundnut processing works here can handle up to 3,000 sacks a day. An old cannon in the village is a reminder of colonial times.

Kuntaur is a busy village clustering on each side of its narrow and dusty main steet. Many of the buildings here are of breeze block instead of the more usual sheet iron, signifying a state of permanence and relative prosperity. The *Lady Denham* was wrecked near here and

Ground nuts waiting for shipment at Fatoto.

is still a hazard to navigation.

A simple bush track leads south-west for six miles to the village of **Barajali,** birthplace of President Jawara, but tourists will be paying more attention to reaching **Wassu** and looking for the stone circles. If you're travelling by public transport your best way of seeing the circles is to get out at Wassu village, just west of the track. The circles are in a walled enclosure just visible over the fields 200 yards to the east. A guardian lives on site, and there's no entry fee — but a tip would be welcome.

Lamin Koto, across the river from Georgetown, is at the limit of up-country travel on the North Bank by bus, thus making bush taxi the only logical way of progressing further — unless you have chartered a Black and White Land-Rover with driver. And if this is the only North Bank village you visit, don't worry: there are some stone circles in the neighbourhood.

At **Karantaba Tenda,** to the east, the Mungo Park memorial stone stands almost on the river bank, and is easier to see from a boat. Further up-country are two villages among many in the country to carry the name **Darsilami** or Dasilami, a local variation of Dar-es-Salaam, 'Palace (or house) of Peace.'

Sutukoba, 'Great Sutuko,' almost at the end of the track, was a town of around 4,000 people in the early 16th cent, a meeting-place for Portuguese traders who came upriver, and African merchants who came overland. The town has long since lost its glory. In the semi-desert country to the north, close to the Senegalese border, the village of **Gunjur Kuta,** 'New Gunjur,' ('Old Gunjur' is in Senegal) has a manually-dug well that is 120 feet deep, showing that this part of The Gambia is in the Sahel, far from the mangrove swamps and bolongs of Banjul, where our journey began.

13: INTO SENEGAL

Casamance delights

THE PEOPLE OF SENEGAL and The Gambia are united by strong tribal bonds, yet they are divided by a sense of nationality that is a legacy from colonial times. Since the collapse of the Senegambia federation, the invisible boundary between the two countries — it's marked by the occasional concrete pillar — has become a political barrier. Before 30 September 1989, Gambian buses and bush taxis crossed the border freely, pausing only to show that they had adequate insurance, and Gambian workers went into Senegal for better-paid jobs, even though the cost of living is much higher.

After that date in 1989, the Senegalese tightened border controls to Gambians, and there are rumours of Gambian women being strip-searched.

European free passage. But none of those frustrations applies to Europeans. If your skin is white, you therefore have money, and you are welcome. Holders of European Community passports do not need **visas** to enter Senegal, although Scandinavians, Americans, Canadians, and Australasians do; they're available at the Senegalese embassy in Banjul for a small fee and two photographs.

Political unrest. As you sit in your smart tourist hotel and contemplate going into Senegal, people will advise you to forget the idea: there's political unrest, rape and pillage, they'll say. But you will also be advised not to consider going up-country in The Gambia: there's no electricity no decent hotel, and the water comes from open wells, they'll say. Of course, when you're not in the hotel you're not spending money there.

My advice on the latter issue is to ignore the advisers; your safari into remote Gambia can be an adventure of a lifetime. Do it. Go. By hire car, by tourist taxi, by public bus, on excursion, but go.

My advice on Senegal is to be a little more cautious, but don't be deterred by people who have not been there. There *is* political unrest; the Casamance Separatist Movement is trying to break away from the remainder of the country and there is a strong and obtrusive military presence in the region. Armoured personnel carriers with machine guns are in every village, and you may hear unsubstantiated rumours of massacres of innocent villagers. But unless you hear

Georgetown's ferry landing-place is a convenient spot for doing the laundry.

genuine stories of border incidents involving Europeans, go. After all, French tour operators are taking package visitors to the smart hotels of Cap Skirring and Kafountine.

Into Senegal. The road crossing into the Casamance is on the tarmac track south from Mandina Ba, east of Brikama, and the frontier post is at Jiboroh. The Gambian exit formalities are simple: your passport is stamped, and the driver of your vehicle pays D5 for a *laissez-passer*. At Seleti in Senegal the customs officer asks for CFA1,200 (£1.20,) to check the laissez-passer, and stamps your passport. You may be asked for *un cadeau,* 'a gift,' but if you decide you cannot speak French the issue is not pursued.

Roads. The roads are good, but not perfect. Into Diouloulou and on to Kafountine on the coast, or inland to Bignona, there are occasional potholes. The Transgambia Highway south to Ziguinchor, and north-east to Soma in The Gambia, has some nasty but localised bad spots. A smart bridge crosses the Casamance River into Ziguinchor, where you will inevitably lose your way due to lack of signposts. Once you find your way out of Ziguinchor the road to Cap Skirring is good, and runs parallel with the border of Guinea Bissau for the last few miles. In 1990-91 *gas oil* (diesel) cost CFA210 per litre (CFA955 or £1.90 per Imperial gallon) and *essence* (petrol, gasoline) cost CFA185 per litre (CFA840 or £1.70 per gallon), slightly cheaper than in The Gambia, although it has historically been more expensive. But you need to pay for it in *ceefas.*

The splendid beach at Cap Skirring in Senegal.

Cap Skirring. The resort of Cap Skirring, Senegal's southernmost point at 12° 19' N, is a small African community with the inevitable mud huts beside several smart tourist hotels, including Club Méditerranée. Access to the vast beach is possible only on foot or by Land-Rover. **Kafountine,** the more popular destination because it is closer to The Gambia, is around the same size and has a few tourist hotels. It is possible to cover the 280 miles (450km) to Cap Skirring and back to Bakau in a day, provided you start at daybreak and are prepared to return after dark.

Frontier crossings after dark. All road frontier posts close at night, but those on the lesser roads shut at sunset for lack of electricity. On my return from the Casamance we drove our Land-Rover slowly past the Senegalese border post at Seleti, and were crawling past the Jiboroh post in The Gambia when a man dressed in civilian clothes hurried out with a torch. He took our passports and stamped them in a candle-lit hut while the woman beside him marked school exercise books. The man said he was working overtime on our behalf and asked us to pay him. We refused on principal, but I have heard reports from other Europeans who paid, and received an official receipt.

The Casamance. The Casamance is a beautiful region, surprisingly different from The Gambia although it is so near. There are more mangrove swamps, more trees, particularly some enormous mahogany specimens, as well as the teak plantations by the Guinea Bissau border, and the bird population is greater. It is an experience not to be missed.

KEY TO BAKAU VILLAGE & BAKAU & SEREKUNDA AREA MAPS ON PAGES 183 (opposite) and 184-185 (overleaf) Entries marked ★ *are better seen on the map opposite.*

HOTELS in the package business:

★ African Village	1
Andalaye Village	2
★ Amie's Beach	3
Badala Park	4
★ Bakotu	5
★ Bungalow Beach	7
★ Cape Point Bungalow	8
★ Fajara	9
★ Fransisco's	10
★ Friendship	11
Holiday Beach	12
Kairaba	13
Kololi Beach Club	14
★ Kombo Beach (Novotel)	15
★ Kotu Strand	16
Palma Rima	17
★ Romana	18
Senegambia Beach	19
★ Sunwing	20
★ Tropic Garden	21

HOTELS, etc, not packaged:

★ Atlantic Guest House	25
Bakadaji Bungalows	26
Bantaba	27
Boucarabou	28
Bunkoyo ᒐ ᔅ3 ᑫ ᔅ/ ᒐᔭ ᗐᑫᒪ	29
Green Line Motel	30
Keneba	31
Kololi Tavern	32
Montrose Holidays	33
Paradise Inn	34
★ Safari Inn	35
★ Sambou's	36

HOTELS, etc, local market:

Gambissara Motel	40
Julakunda	41
Serakunda Motel	42
Serekunda Hotel	43
Verdi Motel	44
★ Wintersun	45
YMCA Hostel	46

SHOPS, EMBASSIES, etc:

★ Atson's Supermarket	50
★ Avis car hire	51
★ Bakau produce market	52
★ Bengdula (tourist market)	53
★ British High Commission	54
Casino, old (closed)	55
★ CFAO supermarket	56
★ Fajara war cemetery	57
★ Foodworth supermarket	58
★ Fritz's car hire	59
★ Gamtel	60
Kololi Casino	61
★ President's residence	62
★ Russian Embassy	63
★ Vice-president's residence	64

Key opposite

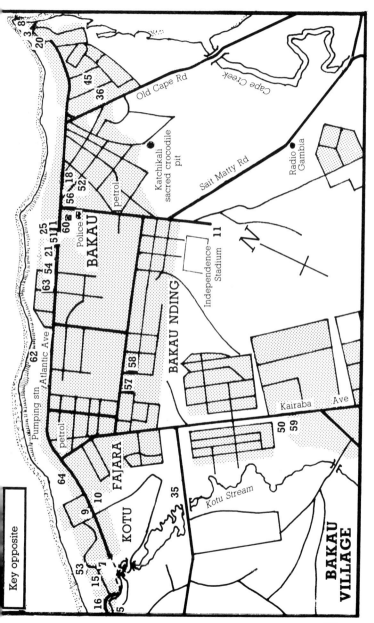

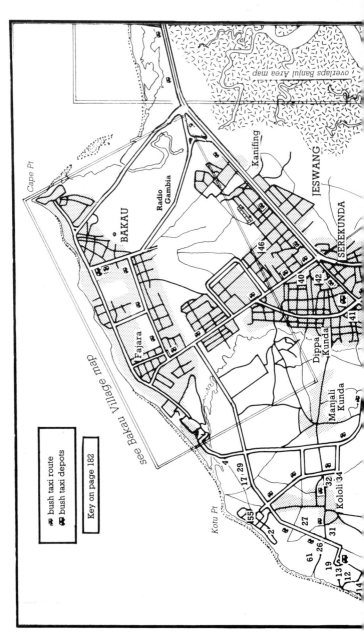

Cape Pt

BAKAU

Fajara

Radio Gambia

Kanifing

IESWANG

SEREKUNDA

Dippa Kunda

Manjali Kunda

Kotu Pt

Kololi

see Bakau Village map

overlaps Banjul Area map

bush taxi route
bush taxi depots

Key on page 182

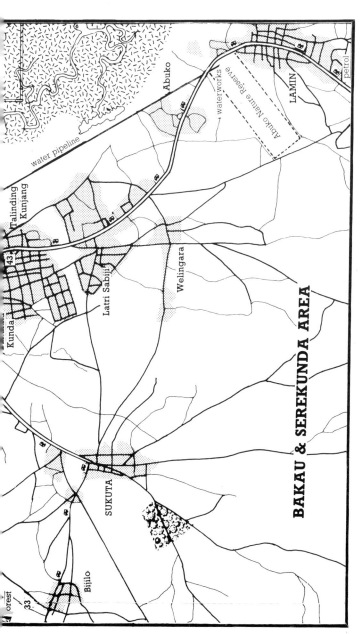

BAKAU & SEREKUNDA AREA

BANJUL: KEY

Albert Market	2
Atlantic Hotel	3
Banks: BICI	6
-Central	7
-Standard Chartered	9
Barra ferry terminal	10
Cathedrals: Anglican	11
-Catholic	12
Catholic Relief Service	13
CFAO supermarket	14
Chapels: Bethel	15
-Wesleyan	16
City Council office	17
College of Nursing	18
Crab Island Sec Sch	19
Embassies: Lebanese	20
-Senegalese	21
Fire Station	22
Gamtel (☎)	23
General Post Office	24
Govt offices: general	25
-Interior Ministry	26
-Information & Tourism	27
Great Mosque (new)	29
Great Mosque (former)	30
High School	
Hotels (not 'tourist'): Apollo	
-Carlton	
-Kantora	
-Teranga	
King George V Mem'l Pk	
Law Courts	
Methodist Bookshop	
National Assembly	
National Museum	
National Trading Corp (NTC)	
Oil storage tanks	
Police barracks	
Police headquarters	
Power station	
Restaurants: African Heritage	
− Braustüble	
− Oasis	
Royal Victorial Hospital	
St Augustine's School	
State House	
Taxi stand	
United Nations office	
Victoria Sports Ground	
War Memorial	

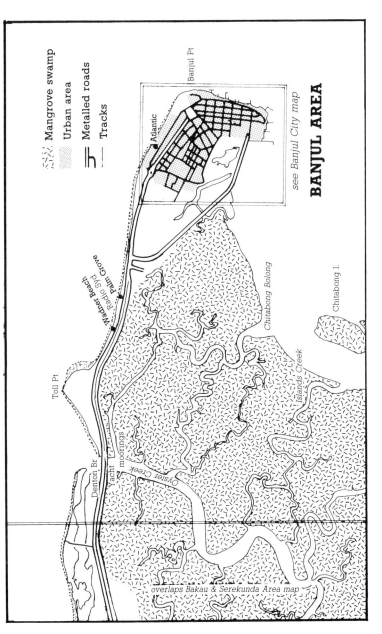

Mangrove swamp
Urban area
Metalled roads
Tracks

BANJUL AREA

see Banjul City map

Banjul Pt

Atlantic

Chitabong Bolong

Islands Creek

Chitabong I.

Wagner Beach

Palm Grove

Radio Syd

Toll Pt

Denton Br

Yacht
moorings

Oyster Creek

overlaps Bakau & Serekunda Area map

187

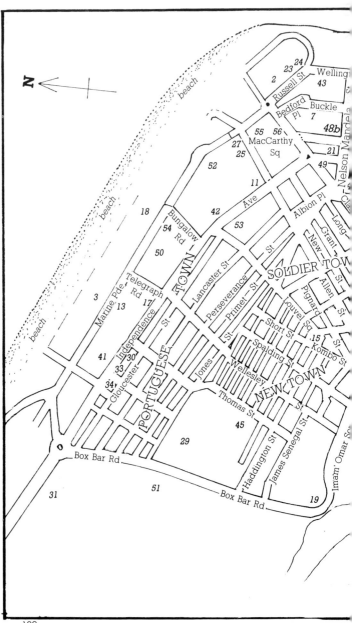

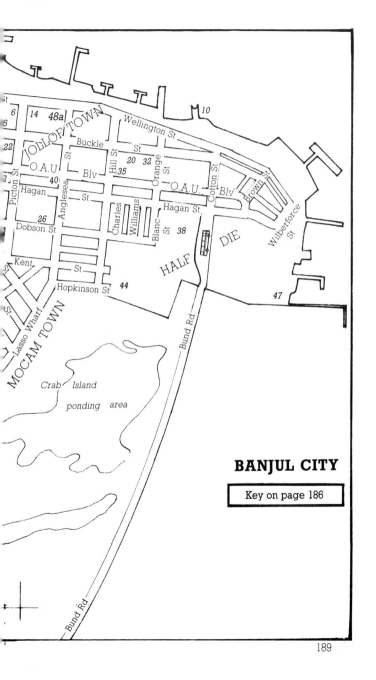

BANJUL CITY

Key on page 186

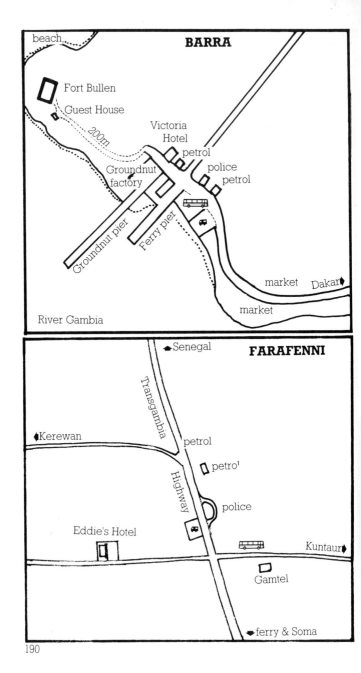

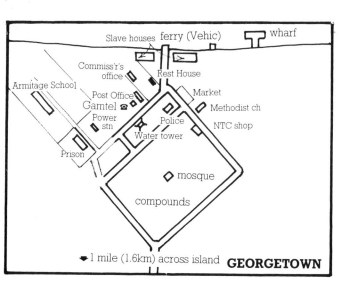

Georgetown map labels:
- Slave houses
- ferry (Vehic)
- wharf
- Commiss'r's office
- Rest House
- Armitage School
- Post Office
- Market
- Gamtel ☎
- Methodist ch
- NTC shop
- Power stn
- Police
- Water tower
- Prison
- mosque
- compounds
- ← 1 mile (1.6km) across island **GEORGETOWN**

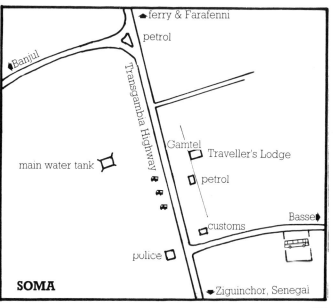

Soma map labels:
- ← ferry & Farafenni
- petrol
- ← Banjul
- Transgambia Highway
- Gamtel
- Traveller's Lodge
- main water tank
- petrol
- customs
- Basse →
- police
- **SOMA**
- ← Ziguinchor, Senegal

191

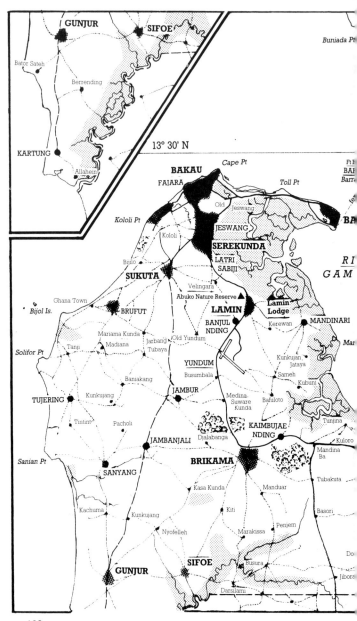

SENEGAL

Duniajoe Sanchi
MBangkama
Njongon
NDofan
let Bah
MBollet NDing
a
ayamba Berending
Buniadu

Amdallai
Tuba
FASS
Medina Manneh
MBullum
Ker Wally
Chamen
Ker MBougouma

Ker Samba Yassin
Maka Bala
Mana
Maka Nien Jam
Bantanding Toranka
Ker Malick Sarr
Omar Jowara
Medina Madum
NDungu Charon Ker Abdou Fady
Ker NGor
Lohen
NDUNGU KEBBE
Ker Gido
Ker Sulleh
Jamagen
Ker Samba Kalla
Sotokoi
Ker Sidyke
Memmeh
Ker Samba Njabeh
Ker Ousman Buso

13° 30' N
MEDINA SERINGE MASS

Ker Biran Kani
Ker Sait Cham
Passi Challi
Chamen Sosseh

Bakendik
Fass Omar Saher
Medina Bafuloto
Prince
Killa

Njambour
Bafulotor

Pakela
Demba Colleh
Sare Mama
Sami Bolong
Jurunku

BAKALARR
Nema Kunku
Aljamdu
Sittanunka
Madina Sacheboe
Sami Bajonkoto

Jereh Kungotu
Tuba Kolong
Pakau Ba
Pakau Penku

d Pt
LAMIN
Juffure
Sika Baduma

Bantang Killing
ALBREDA
▲ Slave House, Juffure
Sika Pt

Lamin Pt
◦ Ft James I.

RIVER GAMBIA

Biara Pt
Bulanjor

Sansankoto I.
Tuba Kuta

ABA ANTA
Bulok
Bolong
Jakoi Sibrik
Batending Kajara
Kassagne

Brefet
Kanuma

Kafuta
Killy

Faraba Soto
Bajana
NDemban Chapechum
SOMITA
Kabokor

Sohm
Sanianga
Sutu Sinjang
BESSI
NDemban Jola
Sandehmunku
Gikis

Kafuta Tumbung
BULOK
Kanjabina
Janack

16° 30' W
SENEGAL

193

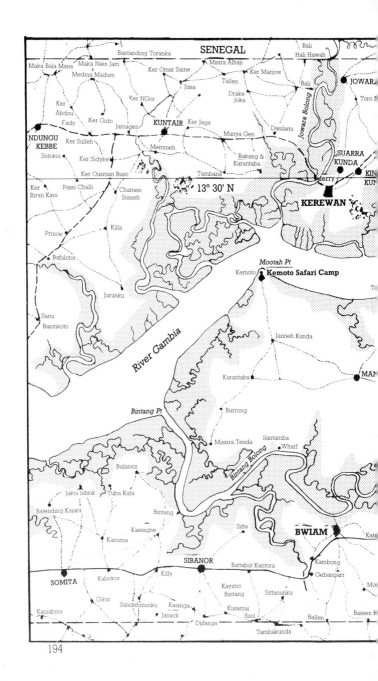

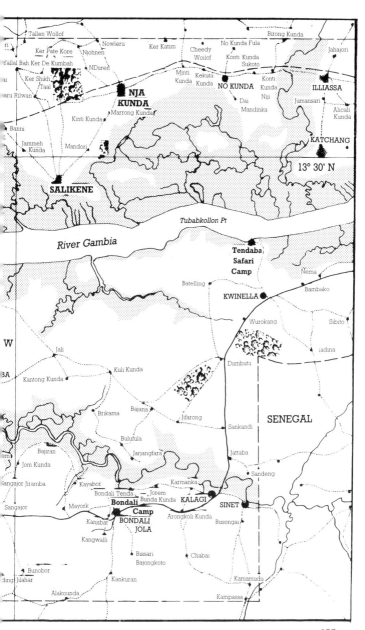

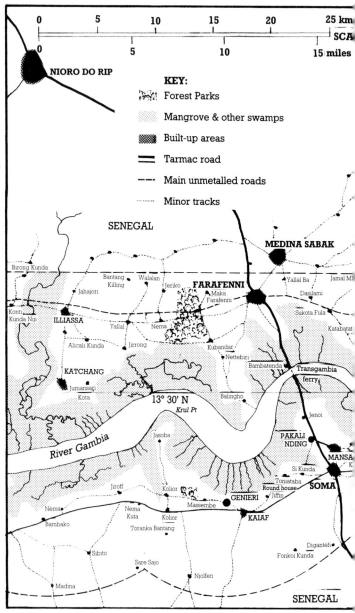

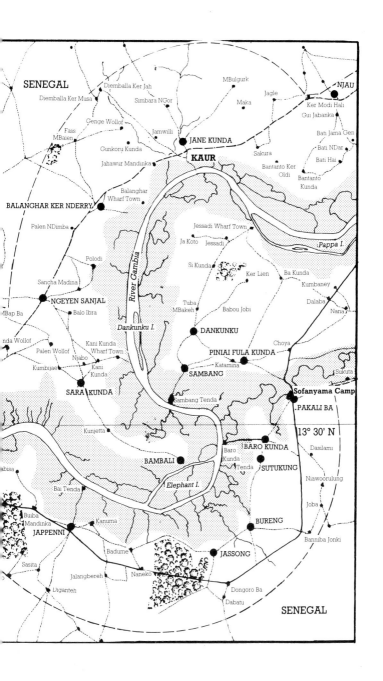

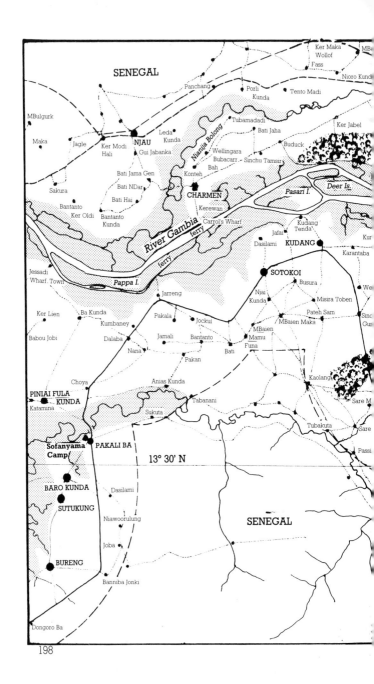

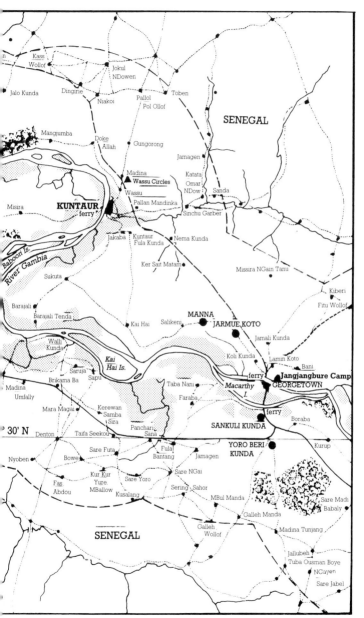

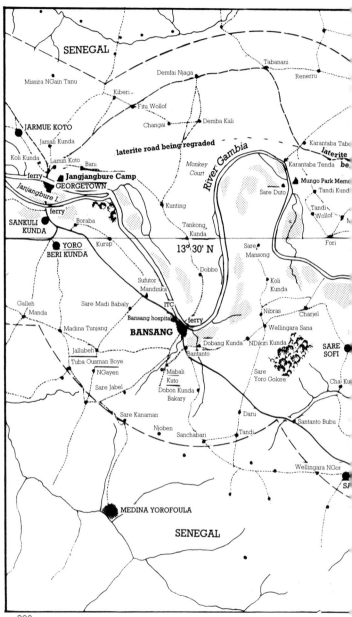

SENEGAL

Missira NGain Tanu

Tabanani

Renerru

Demfai Njaga

Kiberi

Fitu Wollof

JARMUE KOTO

Jamali Kunda

Changai

Demba Kali

Koli Kunda

Lamin Koto

Bani

Karantaba Tabo

laterite road being regraded

laterite

Monkey Court

River Gambia

Karantaba Tenda be

ferry

Jangjangbure Camp
GEORGETOWN

Mungo Park Memo

Janjangbure I.

Sare Duto

Tandi Kund

ferry

Kunting

Tandi
Wollof

SANKULI
KUNDA

Boraba

N

YORO
BERI KUNDA

Kurup

Tankong
Kunda

13° 30' N

Fori

Sare
Mansong

Sufutor
Mandinka

Dobbo

Koli
Kunda

Galleh
Manda

Sare Madi Babaly

ITC

Bansang hospital

ferry

Nibras

Charjel

Madina Tunjang

BANSANG

Wellingara Sana

Jallubeh

Dobang Kunda

NDikiri Kunda

SARE
SOFI

Tuba Ousman Boye

Bantanto

NGayen

Mabali
Kuto

Sare
Yoro Golore

Chai Ku

Sare Jabel

Dobon Kunda
Bakary

Sare Kanaman

Daru

Santanto Bubu

Njoben

Sanchabari

Tandi

Wellingara NGor

S

MEDINA YOROFOULA

SENEGAL

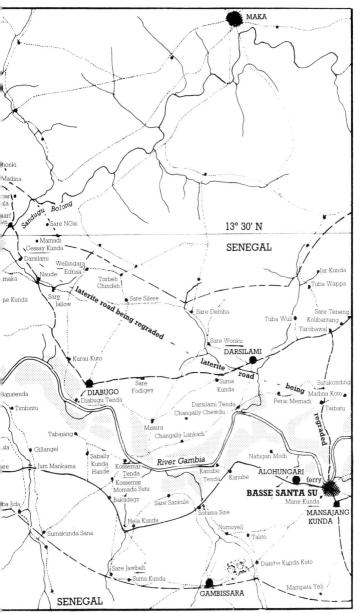

MAKA

nonki

Madina

nar
ula
arf
wn

Sandugu Bolong

Sare NGai

13° 30' N

SENEGAL

Mamadi
Cessay Kunda

Darsilami
Wellingara
Edrisa

maka   Naude

Torbeh
Chindeh

jie Kunda   Sare
Jallow

laterite road being regraded

Sare Silere

Jar Kunda
Tuba Wappa

Sare Demba

Tuba Wuli
Sare Teneng
Kolibantang
Yarobawal

Sare Wonku

DARSILAMI

laterite   road

Kurau Kuto

Banatenda

DIABUGO
Diabugu Tenda

Sare
Fodigey

Suma
Kunda

being

Sutukonding
Madina Koto
Perai Memadi   Taibatu

Darsilami Tenda
Changally Chewdu

regraded

Timbintu

Missira
Changally Lankadi

Tabajang

Gillangel

ula

re   Jum Mankama

Sabally
Kunda
Hande

Kossemar
Tenda

River Gambia

Nafugan Modi

Kanube
Tenda   Kanube

ALOHUNGARI
ferry

ba Jida

Kossemar
Momadu Sutu
Bakadagy

Sare Sankule

BASSE SANTA SU
Mane Kunda

MANSAJANG
KUNDA

Hela Kunda

Sotuma Sire

Sumakunda Sana

Numuyell
Talito

Sare Jawbeh
Suma Kunda

Domba Kunda Kuto

Mampata Yeli

SENEGAL

GAMBISSARA

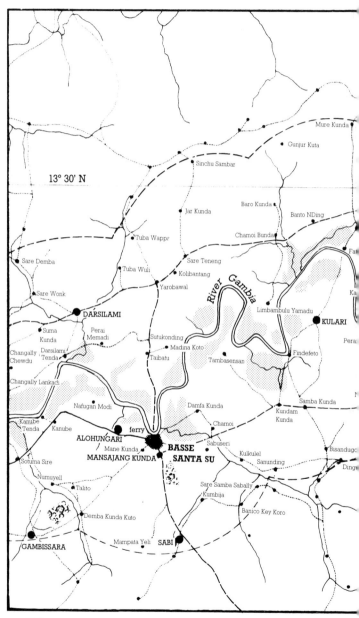

13° 30' N

Mure Kunda

Gunjur Kuta

Sinchu Sambar

Baro Kunda

Banto NDing

Jar Kunda

Chamoi Bunda

Tuba Wappa

Pa

Sare Demba

Sare Teneng

Tuba Wuli

Kolibantang

River Gambia

Yarobawal

Sare Wonk

Ka

Limbambulu Yamadu

DARSILAMI

KULARI

Suma
Kunda

Perai
Memadi

Sutukonding

Perai

Changally
Chewdu

Darsilami
Tenda

Madina Koto

Taibatu

Findefeto

Tambasensan

Changally Lankadi

Nafugan Modi

Damfa Kunda

Samba Kunda

Kanube
Tenda

Kanube

ferry

Chamoi

Kundam
Kunda

ALOHUNGARI

Mane Kunda

Sabuseri

Bisandugo

MANSAJANG KUNDA

**BASSE
SANTA SU**

Kulkulel

Sotuma Sire

Sanunding

Ding

Numuyell

Talito

Sare Samba Sabally

Demba Kunda Kuto

Kumbija

Banico Key Koro

GAMBISSARA

Mampata Yeli

SABI

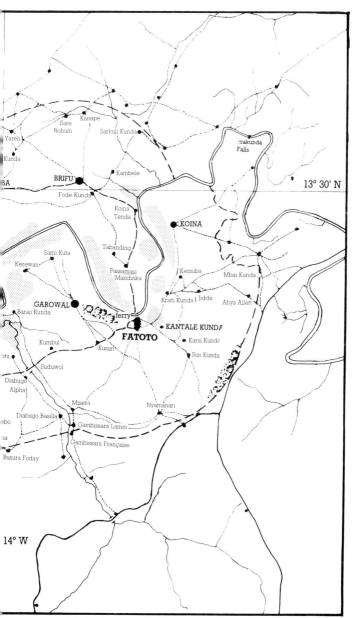

13° 30' N

14° W

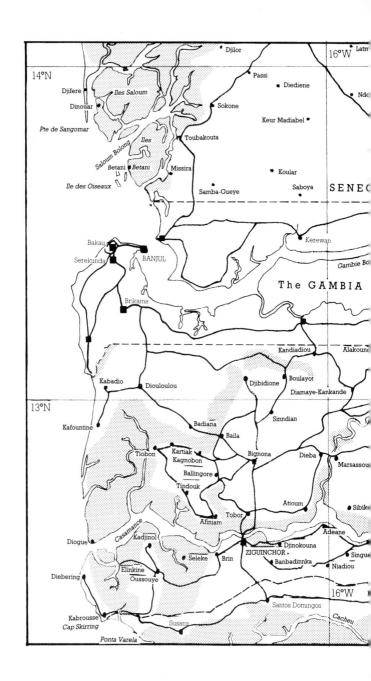

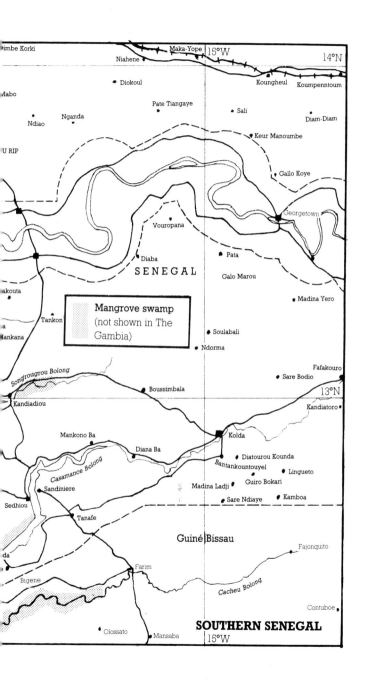

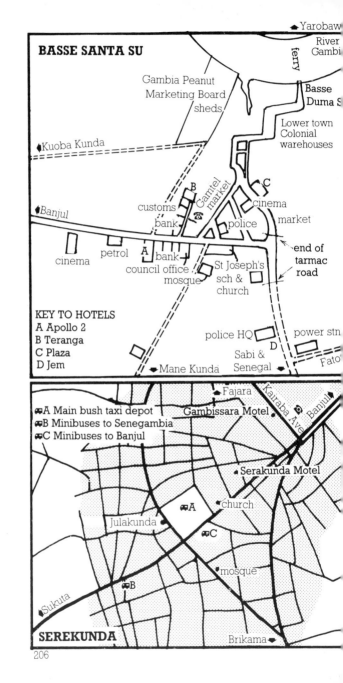

BASSE SANTA SU

Yarobaw▶

River
Gambi

ferry

Basse
Duma S

Gambia Peanut
Marketing Board
sheds

Lower town
Colonial
warehouses

◀Kuoba Kunda

C

B

Camtel market

cinema

customs

◀Banjul

bank

☎

police

market

cinema

petrol

A

bank

end of
tarmac
road

council office

St Joseph's

mosque

sch &
church

KEY TO HOTELS
A Apollo 2
B Teranga
C Plaza
D Jem

police HQ

power stn

D

Sabi &
Senegal

Fato

◀Mane Kunda

🚐A Main bush taxi depot
🚐B Minibuses to Senegambia
🚐C Minibuses to Banjul

Fajara▶

Gambissara Motel▶

Kairaba Ave

Banjul

Serakunda Motel▶

🚐A

church

Julakunda

🚐C

mosque

Sukuta

🚐B

SEREKUNDA

Brikama▶

INDEX

Abuko Nature Reserve 138-139,150
affiliations........................38
Air Gambia 53
Albert Market 105,167
Albreda 101,159,160,176
Amdalaye buses 131
area 7
armed forces.....................35
Baboon Islands 100
Bakau 170
Balanghar 177
banks 18
Banjul 167-170
– Declaration 141,149
Bansang 174
– hospital 25
Barajali..........................178
bargaining.......................57
Barra 176
– War 163
Barrakunda Falls..........100,165,176
bars 113-117
Basse Santa Su...................175
Bathurst 162
begging..........................64
Bintang 172
birdwatching..... 101–104,108,139-149
Black & White Safaris 103-109
Brefet 172
Brewer, Eddie & Stella............139
Brikama 165
buses 66-68,128-131
bush taxis 127-128
business hours..................35-36
Bwiam 172
Cap Skirring 181
car hire.........................36
Casamance 105,179-181
cathedrals 168-169
Cham, Mass.................101,107
charities 23-24
Clarkson, Thomas 161,164
climate 9
compound 8
cost of living 38-41
credit cards...................17-18
crime 57-58
crocodile pits 153,170
cycles, cycling 38,136
Darsilami 178
Denton Bridge.............101,170
disabled.........................26
Dog Island 159,165
dress 19-21
eating out 110-112
education 41
electricity 41
Elephant Island 100
embassies 42
excursions 100-110
Farafenni 176
farming 42

Fatoto 175
fax machines 51
ferries......................132-136
flag 43
food 111-112
Fort Bullen 163
Fort James I. 101,103,159-161
Gambia Airways 53
Gambian Heritage 106-107
Gamtours......................103-9
gas 43
Georgetown 135,163,174,177
Ghana Town 172
gifts..............................23
Government 43
GPTC buses 128-130
groundnuts 166,175
Gunjur 172
– Kuta 178
Haley, Alex 109-110,161
Half Die 168
Harmattan 10
health 11-15
hospitals......................24,44
hotels, etc:
– Adonis Hotel 118
– African Village Hotel 69-70
– Amdalaye Village Hotel 71
– Amie's Beach Hotel 71
– Apollo Hotel 118
– Apollo 2 Hotel.................126
– Atlantic Guest House 119
– Atlantic Hotel 7-73
– Badala Park Hotel 73-74
– Bakadaji Bungalows.............119
– Bakotu Hotel 74-75
– Bantaba Hotel 75
– Bondali Camp..................96
– Boucarabou Hotel 75-76
– Bungalow Beach Hotel 76-77
– Bunkoyo Hotel 119
– Cape Point Bungalow Hotel 78
– Carlton Hotel 119
– Clive & Marcia's Place 120
– Commissioner's Guest Houses:
––– Bansang....................125
––– Georgetown 125
––– Mansa Konko 124
– Eddie's Hotel, Farafenni 124
– Fajara Hotel 78-79
– Fankanta Hotel 125
– Follonko Guest House 120
– Fransisco's Hotel 80
– Friendship Hotel 80-81
– Gambissara Motel 120
– Government Rest Ho, Barra 121
– Green Line Motel..............121
– I.T.C., Bansang 125
– Jangjangbure Camp 99-100
– Jem Hotel, Basse 126
– Julakunda Hotel 121
  Kairaba Hotel 82-83
– Kantora Hotel 121
– Kemoto Camp..................98
– Keneba Hotel 121

– Kololi Beach Club 83-84
– Kololi Tavern 122
– Kombo Beach Hotel 84-85
– Kotu Strand Hotel 85-86
– Linguere Motel 126
– Montrose Holidays 122
– Novotel 84
– Palma Rima Hotel 87
– Palm Grove Hotel 87-89
– Paradise Inn 123
– Plaza Hotel, Basse 126
– Romana Hotel 89
– Safari Inn 90
– Sambou's Hotel 90
– Senegambia Beach Hotel 91-92
– Serakunda Motel 123
– Serekunda Hotel 123
– Sofanyama Camp 98-99
– Sunwing Hotel 93
– Tendaba Camp 96-98,103,173
– Teranga Hotel, Banjul 123
– Teranga Hotel, Basse 126
– Traveller's Lodge, Bansang 125
– Traveller's Lodge, Pakali NDing . . 124
– Traveller's Lodge, Soma 124
– Tropic Garden Hotel 93-94
– Victoria Hotel, Barra 123
– Wadner Beach Hotel 94-95
– Y.M.C.A. Hostel 123
independence 166
independent travel 15-16,22-24
Jamond 100
Juffure 103,176
Kafountine 105,181
Kalaji 172
Kantaba 177
Karaba Tenda 118
Kaur 177
Keneba 172
Kerewan 176
Kristi Kunda 175
Kuntaur 177
Lady Chilel 164
Lamin Koto 178
Lamin Lodge 96
language 7,29-34
MacCarthy, Col Charles 162
Mali Kingdom 157
Mansa Konko 174
maps 44-45
money 17-9
Mosque, Great 170
motoring laws 37
mumbo-jumbo 161
Museum 169
newspapers 45
nightlife 117
oil reserves 40
overland travel 54
Pappa Island 100
Park, Mungo 106,161-162,178
passports 9
petrol 37
photography 21,59-61
police 46,60-62
Polygamy 33
population 46-47
Post Office 36,47,165
Prester John 158
property, buying of 50
prostitution 58-59
public holidays 47-48
– toilets 48
radio 48-49
rainfall 10
religion 27-28
residence 49-50
restaurants 113-117
river cruises 100
– steamers 164
roads 132
Roots 109-110
safari camps 96-100
St Mary's I 162,165
St Mawes Castle 100
sea travel 54
self-catering 21
Senegal 179-81
Senegambia Federation 166
Serekunda 171
Sierra Leone 162
slavery 110,157-159
Songhai 157
Soniki-Marabout War 165,173
souvenirs 62
Spirit of Galicia 100
sports 51
Sunshine Holidays 103-9
sun's zenith 10
Sutukoba 178
Tanji 172
Tankular 173
taxis, bush 127-128
– tourist 31,38
telephones 51-52
television 49
time 52
tipping 62
Toniataba 173
toubab 64
tourist guides 63-64
– offices 16
– season 25-27
Transgambia Highway 133
up-country travel 126-138
video cameras 61
visas 9,179
Wassu Circles 100,156,178
water 15
weights & measures 52
West African Tours 103-9
Wilberforce, William 161,164
women alone 26
wrestling 51,104
Yundum Airport 53-54,17
Zuguinchor 106,180